Lean transformation is a socio-political process!

Jeff K[signature]

Lean transformation is a socio-political process!

TRENCHES

BY JEFFREY K. LIKER

The Toyota Way
The Toyota Way Fieldbook (w/David Meier)
The Toyota Product Development System (w/James Morgan)
Becoming Lean (w/James Womack)
Toyota Under Fire (w/Timothy Ogden)
Toyota Culture (w/Mike Hoseus)
Developing Lean Leaders at All Levels (w/Ron Carter)
The Toyota Way to Lean Leadership (w/Gary Convis)
Remade in America (w/W. Mark Fruin)
Engineered in Japan (w/John Ettie)
Concurrent Engineering Effectiveness (w/Mitchell Fleischer)
Kaizen for the Shopfloor Learning Package

BY JEFFREY K. LIKER and JAMES K. FRANZ

The Toyota Way to Continuous Improvement

Copyright © 2016 by James K. Franz & Jeffrey K. Liker
All rights reserved.
ISBN-13: 978-1530511211
ISBN-10: 1530511216

TRENCHES

A LEAN TRANSFORMATION NOVEL

JAMES K. FRANZ

JEFFREY K. LIKER

In Loving Memory

For Mary Kay: an avid and voracious reader, well-versed and infinitely curious, she was never more than arms-length from any number of books. Gone too soon, this one's for you mom…

Preface

Why should you read this book? Why should you read any book? Typically we read for one of two reasons, either we're trying to deepen our understanding of some issue or another, or we are reading simply for pleasure. In this book we were trying to create something that would give you two for the price of one.

The shelves are overflowing with books about lean management. The challenge for any new book on lean is to find a way to continue to add to the body of material surrounding lean transformation and operational excellence. Otherwise, this would just be a rehash of existing work and wouldn't add any value: Muda in the truest sense and a definite no-no in our line of work. So, we tried to look back over sixty years of collective experience between the two of us, in the trenches, and find some commonalities that we could build upon. After some discussion, we identified a few common threads.

1. **ROI in Search of a toolkit**—Without fail, any of the companies that we come in contact with ask us the same question: "Can you describe to me a company in *exactly* our space that has been on the journey for about five years and what have they experienced?" We can only assume that they want to run some numbers, calculate a quick ROI, and then decide if they want to put together a 'project team' to 'lean out their operations.' We wish them well, but we tell them we can't help them, mostly because they've already set in their mind the path they want to take, the rough order of magnitude resource calculations, and some kind of contribution to the bottom line of the company. Unfortunately, in this all too common scenario, these companies have it exactly

backwards. The tools do not create the ROI. Highly developed people, *using* the right tools, do... routinely.

2. **The War in the Trenches**—The great mass of lean change agents who are in the trenches feel like they are at war with the dominant way of thinking of those with power. There are black belts who believe they are the only ones qualified to drive performance improvement. There are the short-sighted managers who want results, *now*, without an investment in developing people. There is the instability of the company which can change hands at a whim leading to a new regime with its own 'one best way' to achieve business results. And there are senior managers who do not spend enough time in the workplace, the Gemba, to know what is really going on and do not take responsibility for continuous improvement done right.

3. **The 1 inch Deep Problem**—Because of the above, most lean deployments turn into rapid tool implementation so it looks on the surface like "we are world class." Value stream maps, A3 reports, daily management KPIs, standard work sheets, and more clutter the walls. But the lack of people development leaves these as simply nothing more than interesting-looking wall decorations. The company is going 1 inch deep and a mile wide in lean deployment, instead of 1 inch at a time wide and a mile deep.

4. **Lack of team member engagement**—"We have done cool lean projects and have gotten great business results but we cannot get supervisors involved. They are stuck in the past. Workers want to do their job and not waste brain cells on solving our problems."

How can one book solve all these problems, and cheer up frustrated change agents everywhere? The answer is that it cannot. But a well-written novel can engross you in another world where you can identify with the problems they face and get ideas for how to advance your journey.

We've created a small, sheltered microcosm where we can observe one company's journey down the path of transformation toward excellence. While all of the characters and situations are fictional, they should feel familiar. In fact, some of you, our friends and colleagues, should actually recognize yourselves in this work, but don't worry, we won't tell anyone. We wanted you to feel like you were walking alongside this group as they traveled, stumbled, fell, and picked themselves up again, on their own journey toward operational excellence. We tried to distill all of the challenges, both internal and external, that groups of people will face and show you *one* path through the wilderness. Your path may be similar to, or may have been entirely different from, the one we describe here. We're not trying to provide the 'one true way' or '16 things you must do to get lean,' rather we're showing you a *possible* way, complete with all of the trials and tribulations that come along with the effort.

Make no mistake, the journey is never easy, and transformation efforts are a full-contact sport. But take heart, as many before you have walked the path that you're walking now. There have been successes and failures, and that's not the objective. You'll never 'get there.' You will, however, continue to strive to be excellent and along the way you'll develop skills and abilities that you thought were beyond your reach. As you achieve each challenging, higher level of performance, you'll be adding invaluable experience to your personal arsenal.

So with that behind us, we encourage you to get in, sit down, buckle up, hang on, and enjoy the ride.

All the best on your journey,

James K. Franz and Jeffrey K. Liker

```
TDSTMP:    042516.1200Z
PRTY:      STANDARD

SNDR:      KOROMO BASE

TRGT:      GHQ

SITREP:    REGULAR PATROLS OUT
           FROM FIREBASES ALPHA
           AND BRAVO. CONSTRUCTION
           OF FIRE BASES DELTA AND
           ECHO ON SCHEDULE. FIREBASE
           CHARLIE FORTIFICATION
           CONTINUES. ENEMY MOVEMENT
           DETECTED MULTIPLE SECTORS.

[END TRANSMISSION]
```

Epilogue

Johann "Jack" Hartmann stood alone in the empty conference room looking out of the floor-to-ceiling windows across the east lot of the property. Jack was trim, of average height with brown hair and light blue eyes. Cradled in his hands was his third steaming cup of coffee in a battered and chipped mug bearing the Amalgamated company logo. Jack always liked to spend some quiet time in this particular conference room as it was generally shunned by others as it hadn't yet had the benefit of the renovation that was sweeping the rest of the office areas. While the appointments were rather pedestrian, with turn of the century furniture and a battered old mahogany table that looked more suited to an old English manor house, Jack didn't come here to sit, but rather to stand in front of the glass and take in the expansive view of the eastern sky as the sun was just beginning to rise. It was a perfect place to reflect and to plan the day's efforts. The massive cottonwoods that, along with other oaks and maples, made up the natural eastern border to the property swayed gently in the early spring breeze while the sunlight provided a hypnotic mosaic pattern along the freshly cut grass. The trees were all heavy with buds, getting ready to spring forth with the life and rejuvenation that was spring time. With all of the daily pressures and tumult, it was very refreshing to have a place to come and just think; even if it was for a just a little while.

The door opened quietly and the overhead lights dutifully clicked on when the sensor detected the motion. Jack typically stood still enough while he drank his coffee and became lost in his own thoughts that the motion detector would turn off the lights after the programmed five minute interval. He took it as a challenge to keep the lights off during his visit.

"G-day Jack, thought I'd find you here. You ready?" asked Tony McAllister, Amalgamated's outside consultant, or 'sensei.' McAllister was Australian, an inch shorter than jack and about ten pounds heavier with close-cropped thinning blonde hair and brown eyes. He spoke with a strong accent peppered occasionally with Cornish rhyming slang, which always required some translation.

Jack turned to see Tony in his standard grey shop coat, fatigue cap and clutching his full size day timer to his chest like protective armor, his safety glasses perched atop his head.

"Sure, why not?" Replied Jack as he turned from his favorite view to join Tony and begin the day.

"But I've got to admit, Tony, that I'm still stuck on the latest assignment you gave me regarding how we continue to move forward here beyond the basic approach that we're using for the Improvement Kata and Coaching Kata. I'm still struggling a bit with the whole cycle of learning. I don't even know if I'll recognize when we get to the next level. I might screw up and hold the teams back. It's frustrating." Jack had a slight headache just starting at the base of his skull. He usually got it when Tony gave him one of his 'learning assignments' which usually boiled down to challenging Jack to think deeper about a problem that Jack didn't even know *was* a problem. Tony was the kind of consultant that used to drive Jack crazy, with answers to questions being met with more questions until, massively frustrated and usually with a pounding headache, a light went on somewhere deep in his skull. It didn't help that any revelation or progress that Jack made was usually met with an ambivalent shrug and another 'assignment.' Jack at first wasn't thrilled with Tony's approach but the more time went by and the more he realized he didn't know about process improvement and people development, he thanked his lucky stars that the fates brought their two paths together. He had learned so much and was desperately hungry for more as the new fiscal year was now well under way.

"No worries mate, tell me where your head is now and let's get down to the daily review with the team in Business Unit 6. I want to see what a brilliant coach I've been training. How are your sister's billy lids?"

They walked out of the conference room and down the hallway to the stairwell that would take them out to the production floor. Jack's thoughts drifted back to the merger that doubled Amalgamated's size almost overnight and kicked off his journey more than a year ago. Was it already a year, no, more than that he thought to himself as he descended the stairs, his steel shanked boots ringing off the metal staircase as he followed Tony out the door, both men pulling down their safety glasses as they headed to the assembly area for the daily review led by the production team leader. Time sure flies, Jack mused, and it's almost unbelievable what happened since the merger announcement. Fourteen months have already slipped by. Yes, it *has* been fourteen months, he confirmed to himself.

But my lord, what a fourteen months...

```
TDSTMP:    030215.0800Z
PRTY:      STANDARD

SNDR:      KOROMO BASE

TRGT:      GHQ

SITREP:    REGULAR PATROLS OUT
           FROM FIREBASES ALPHA,
           BRAVO, AND CHARLIE. NO
           ENEMY MOVEMENT DETECTED.

[END TRANSMISSION]
```

Chapter 1

March 2, 2015

The financial press was still digesting the news this morning and trying to figure out what, if anything, had changed in the reporting that they had done on Friday regarding last week's merger announcement between Shiloh Manufacturing and Amalgamated Industries. The resulting company was dubbed Amalgamated Wood Products reflecting the streamlining of the two companies focus and their future direction. The talking heads on the mainstream outlets were praising the merger and were falling over themselves trying to remember when they first thought that these two companies were candidates ripe for merger. When this line of reporting quickly bore no fruit, the media then began focusing on when the newly formed Amalgamated was going to go public. It was only logical, you see.

"Okay gang, let's head down and see how our pilot line is faring," said Jack.

"Just finishing up pulling last week's summary data big boss man." Replied Kelli O'Malley, one of Jack's Senior Lean Specialists and an old friend. The two had met ten years prior, when Kelli was a freshly minted young engineer and Jack was serving as the engineering leader for a new product launch. Despite Kelli's rather short stature, she was a bit over five feet tall with sandy blonde hair usually in a pony-tail and hazel eyes; Jack quickly learned that she cast a far longer shadow than her size would suggest. She was very sharp with almost total recall and couldn't be intimidated under any circumstances, which was an advantage at her first company, which didn't have what could in any way be called a 'progressive' culture. She was usually smiling and had an infectious laugh. Her sharpness and acumen were strengths that Jack both admired and leaned on at times. During that first launch, so long ago, there were numerous times when Jack and the team came under fire for their insistence on taking enough time to ensure quality before, as one manager indelicately put it, 'shooting the damn engineers and letting 'er rip.' Events bore out the team's approach, as the product launch was generally regarded as one of the best the company had ever had.

Kelli frequently had to back up Jack's arguments with recollections of data or relevant facts that Jack didn't have instant access to. Jack's standard response to demands to 'move faster' was to dig his heels in and proclaim that he would not 'rush things just to make a timing chart look better for some staff bureaucrat.' Kelli then dubbed Jack her favorite 'stubborn sauerkraut.'

Jack left that company and joined another small mid-west manufacturer for over a decade before taking his current job as the Lean Leader of Amalgamated Industries. Kelli was already working at Amalgamated and played a large part in convincing Jack to join the company and help guide their Lean journey. That was just over a month ago.

"Do you want me to come?" Asked Thanh Van Dinh, the newest addition to Jack's team. "Of course," said Jack, "we do all of our line reviews as a team. You can see how we do things and tell me what you used to do over at Shiloh."

"Ok." Thanh replied with a smile as he grabbed his tablet and safety glasses. Thanh was first-generation Vietnamese American and was Jack's height, but was rail thin with dark eyes and a western-style haircut swept up, Jack surmised, with a fair amount of hair gel.

"It looks like they had a good week" said Kelli, looking at the printout in her hand. "They hit their production numbers, mostly, defects are below trend, and they didn't have to run too much overtime."

"Well, that's promising," offered Jack, "I know that Charlie was a bit hesitant to let us work with his team to re-engineer Assembly Line 4 as the pilot line, so I'm glad we're showing some positive results."

* * *

'Charlie' was Charlie Cooks, the Manufacturing Manager for Amalgamated Industries. It was rumored that after the merger with Shiloh was complete he was going to be tapped to oversee all production operations for the merged company. A giant of a man, standing six feet seven inches and weighing in at two hundred and seventy pounds with hands large enough to palm a bowling ball, Charlie had worked his way up through the ranks at Amalgamated from a rail yard laborer through supervisory positions until he sat atop the manufacturing hierarchy at Amalgamated. Charlie grew up on the poorer side of Cleveland and dropped out of high school to find a job to try and bring more money into the Cooks' household. His job search eventually took him to Amalgamated Industries, where after one look at his immense size, he was already north of six feet at fourteen years of age, the rail yard supervisor hired him on the spot. As a young black man working a laborer job, Charlie was the constant target of harassment and hazing from his older co-workers. Knowing how important it was to his family to have his job and the additional income it brought, Charlie learned to let the taunts and slights of his older peer group go unchallenged. He managed to get along for his first two years with Amalgamated. His luck ran out, however, one day during the fall when the leaves on the trees were ablaze in their autumn ritual. Two of Charlie's older workmates came back from lunch smelling of cheap liquor and stale cigarettes and decided it was time to teach the 'young punk' a lesson he wouldn't forget.

"Hey, puke, get over here," said Tom Jorgensen, the senior hourly rail hand.

"Why?" asked Charlie, knowing that Tom and his fellow troublemaker, Mark Williams, were looking for a fight.

"Don't you sass me boy, get your ass over here, now!" barked Tom.

Charlie walked over to where Tom and Mark were standing and stood in front of them, a full head taller than both men and steeling himself for what he knew was coming.

"Go back into the locker room and get me a fresh pair of gloves," said Tom.

"Yeah, I need some fresh ones too" added Mark, clearly slurring his words and reeking of alcohol.

"Go get 'em yourself, drunk fools" said Charlie as he turned to walk away from the confrontation.

"Hey!" yelled Tom, "Don't you turn your back to me you smart-assed little punk"

Charlie kept walking away when Tom and Mark lunged at him, hitting him in the back and knocking him into the dirt next to the rail lines that supplied Amalgamated with all of their raw timber.

"Get up!" screamed Mark, with a vicious look on his purpling face, his fists clenched and spittle on the sides of his mouth.

Charlie stood up and slowly started dusting the dirt from his overalls.

"Leave me alone" he said as he looked first at Mark and then Tom. "I'm not looking for any trouble."

"Well boy, looks like you found some, didn't you?" said Tom as Mark lunged at Charlie and threw a wild haymaker towards Charlie's jaw.

Charlie took a half step back and easily avoided the blow as Mark's momentum took him stumbling over the railroad ties where he tripped and fell face first into the stone road bed. Tom lunged at Charlie and tackled him around the waist trying to take him to the ground. Charlie reached high over his head and brought down his closed fists onto Tom's back and the drunken assailant let out a grunt and crumpled to the ground at Charlie's feet.

"You gonna pay for that boy" Charlie heard from behind him as Mark slowly got up, blood streaming from multiple cuts on his face courtesy of his head-first lunge into the stones and railroad ties. He was pulling a length of pipe from his overalls and advancing menacingly toward Charlie, who was slowly backing up toward the receiving dock doors. A crowd had gathered to witness the spectacle but Charlie noticed no-one was coming to his aid.

Mark flew at Charlie, swing the pipe in a wide arc aimed at his head. Charlie threw up his left arm and crouched low on his right foot to try and avoid the blow. The pipe smashed into his left bicep with a sickening thud. Charlie roared in pain, clenched his massive right hand into a fist the size of a wrecking ball and threw a wicked left cross at Mark that connected directly under his left eye. Mark's head snapped violently around and he fell to the ground like a marionette with its strings cut and lay still.

Charlie looked again to the crowd assembled at the receiving dock and scanned the faces. Somewhere from within the crowd he heard a voice yell "Behind you!" Charlie started to turn just as a white hot explosion of pain rocked his lower back and he fell to his knees. Tom was back on his feet and had hit Charlie square in the kidney from behind with his own pipe: a blow that was intended to break the young man's spine. Charlie's vision was swirling with agony as he rocked back to his feet and whirled to face his assailant.

"I'm gonna split yer stupid head wide open for that, boy!" screamed Tom as he swung backhand at Charlie's head. Charlie stopped the blow with his left hand and pain exploded from his bicep, deeply bruised or broken from Mark's earlier attack. Charlie's massive hand closed around Tom's wrist and wrenched it to the left, spinning Tom sideways and throwing him off balance. Charlie took a half step forward, hurling a punch at Tom's nose. His aim was off, and instead caught Tom right on the side of the jaw, which shattered in a crunch as Tom spun around and hit the ground in a geyser of dust and blood. He, like Mark, lay still on the cold ground.

Charlie stood there for a moment with his hands on his knees, chest heaving and left arm throbbing, looking at the two now unconscious men lying in the dirt. He slowly stood up, brushed himself off and walked back toward the receiving dock. The assembled crowd parted to let him through as he walked back toward the Medical department to have his arm tended to and see how badly his back was injured.

"Anybody else need some damn gloves?" he asked no-one in particular. The assembled crowed was silent.

After the receiving yard incident, nobody bothered Charlie and he was able to do his job without trouble. Charlie was more than just a laborer though, as he took great pains to learn his job and the jobs of his co-workers. His hard work and dedication got him noticed by the management team and he was promoted to senior receiving dock laborer after his third year at Amalgamated. Not long after, after he had gone to night school to complete his high school equivalency exam, Amalgamated Industries promoted Charlie to supervisor, his first management assignment. Over the ensuing years and decades, Charlie methodically worked his way up the management ladder until he reached his goal, running the entire manufacturing operation at Amalgamated. He was considered firm but fair, a great boss to work for until you tried to pull some shenanigans or didn't deliver on something you had promised. An agitated Charlie Cooks was fearsome to behold.

* * *

"Hey Jolly Green, how's it going?" asked Kelli as she looked up at Charlie, who was standing at the Production Control board.

"Now who could that be? I hear a voice but I don't see anybody" Charlie said, as he turned around, shielded his eyes against a non-existent sun and looked dramatically over Kelli's head to the left and to the right.

"Oh! It's Short Round!" said Charlie, finally looking down at Kelli. "How nice of you to join us this morning." He dutifully bent down to receive one of Kelli's mandatory hugs. She then playfully jabbed him in the ribs, which was about as high as she could reach on him. He winked and smiled and then turned to address the rest of the group.

"Morning Jack" said Charlie as his outstretched hand completely enveloped Jack's. Please don't squeeze too hard, thought Jack.

"And this must be young Thanh, the whiz kid from Shiloh."

Thanh stepped forward and sheepishly stuck his hand out, fearful that the towering Charlie would return it with a compound fracture or two. Or eight.

"Please to meet you sir," said Thanh, quietly, as he looked at something in the general direction of Kelli's shoes.

"Don't worry son, my bark is worse than my bite," said Charlie as he gingerly shook Thanh's hand. "And don't believe half the stuff Kelli says about me. She's a troublemaker through and through."

Kelli rolled her eyes and shook her head, which brought a brief smile to Thanh's face.

"Ok," began Charlie, "let's talk about how this pilot line has been doing. I gotta say, I didn't think it was a good idea to take our most profitable line and put it up as the guinea pig for you and your team. But, looking at how it's coming along and talking it over with our team members and supervisors, I'm not ashamed to admit I was wrong. The change has been pretty impressive."

"I'm glad," said Jack. "Your team has done the lion's share of the work and we've still got a lot ahead of us after the weeklong re-engineering workshop we did a few weeks back."

"I know what they did. I also know what they're capable of," said Charlie with a smile. "You got the latest numbers on the line short round?"

"Yep, see for yourself. Everything has been moving in the right direction all week, even though you got hit with all of the high content product lines," said Kelli as she handed over a fresh copy of the schedule and the financial performance for the line.

Charlie perched a pair of reading glasses on the end of his nose and looked up and down the financial summary sheet that Kelli had printed and then began to look back and forth between the schedule and the summary. Without a word to the group he started walking over to the pilot area and motioned over Geoff Mueller, the business unit leader. From a distance Jack, Kelli, and Thanh could see Charlie gesturing back and forth from the line to the charts. He was obviously grilling Geoff on last week's performance. Jack was beginning to feel a bit uneasy when Charlie came striding back to the group with a perplexed look on his face. He kept walking past the assembled group and stopped again in front of the Production Control Board. He began tracing his finger between the various reports and graphs and looking back at the results from last week in his hand. Jack and the team walked over and gathered around Charlie and waited.

"Well I'll be…" said Charlie in a quiet voice. He stood up and turned around to look at Jack and the assembled group, which now included Geoff as he had walked over from Assembly Line 4 to see what had his boss's boss so energized.

"Jack, it looks like everything jibes here. Geoff," said Charlie looking at his business unit leader, "you're confident that our new team leader structure on this line is why we've been able to absorb that crazy schedule and still keep knockin' 'em out of the park?"

"100% confident boss, if we didn't have those team leaders in place, all of our re-engineering work would have already started coming undone. My supervisors on both shifts have been unanimous on this one with zero negative feedback. The girls and guys on the line now have a real lifeline and can get the help they need without having to walk out of the area to get help," replied Geoff. Geoff and Jack looked like they came from the same mold, with both having a similar build and hair color. Kelli joked that they were probably separated at birth.

"And," continued Charlie, "It looks like the training is happening." With this, Geoff beamed. "But, it looks like we're a bit behind schedule on the training, so Geoff, I'd like to know by this afternoon how you're going to get back on schedule." Geoff's smile quickly vanished as he looked up into Charlie's stern visage. After holding his gaze for a few long seconds, Charlie smiled and clapped Geoff on the shoulder. "Relax son, we're behind but I'm pretty confident you can get us back on track. Talk it over with your supervisors and I'm sure everything can be put right."

"Thanks Charlie, will do." With that Geoff headed back, double-time, to the area to convene a brief meeting with his supervisors.

Charlie watched him go, knowing that they'd begin discussing what needed to be done to achieve their training plan. He smiled, knowing that the culture he had spent a lifetime building centered on the simple theme of 'what's wrong with right now?'

"Penny for your thoughts Jolly…" said Kelli, looking up at Charlie, who was staring blankly in the general direction of Assembly Line 4.

"Hmm? Oh, nothing much." said Charlie, looking down at Kelli and giving her a big smile. "Come on Short Round, why don't you buy me a coffee?"

"Fine, fine. Big Mr. Got-Rocks and he needs poor old Kelli to buy him some java. Let's go," and with that they headed to the plant's canteen area for a cup of steaming coffee.

"Thanh," Jack said, "Come here and take a look at the Production Control board for Line 4. This was our pilot line. We focused all of our efforts and training in this one area so we could better understand the needs of the people and the processes. We used a pretty standard lean approach and created Current and Future State Value Stream maps. Prior to the workshop we were able to get good representation from all of the departments. Production, Quality, Maintenance, and Logistics all had knowledgeable people with us for the week. Then we broke the future state into loops and began the do process loop by loop, process by process—broke down the elephant into smaller bites.

"That sounds like a great approach," said Thanh, "typically at Shiloh we just have our internal lean team work on a project deck and we made sure that there was an accountability mechanism. Our certified Master Lean Six Sigma Sensei were the drivers of the program."

"Hmm," said Jack, "how did you feel about the work you were doing?"

"Well, the technical part of the improvements were fairly easy. It was just basic Industrial Engineering work with a lot of data crunching. That was my area of expertise, the data."

"How did the improvements go?"

"Initially they were very effective, but over time some of the gains were lost. Sustainability was always a challenge."

"Agreed," said Jack, "we've always had the same challenges. With the pilot area approach, we're working through Charlie and the whole team and we guarantee we will give them continued support and attention until they build up the necessary skills to maintain the new standards without external support."

"I imagine that Mr. Cooks appreciates that approach," said Thanh.

"Charlie supported us pretty strongly once he heard what we were trying to do and how we were going to do it," replied Jack.

"I can't imagine," said Thanh, with a bit of awe, "that much would get done without Charlie's full support."

"I guarantee that Thanh, but it's better for you to see it in action. Let's head over for the daily management meeting and I'll introduce you to the rest of the leadership team here at Amalgamated."

With that, Jack and Thanh headed down the main aisle to the conference room next the plant manager's office. The sounds of the factory faded behind them as the thick fireproof door separating the shop floor from the offices slowly closed and clicked shut.

```
TDSTMP:     031615.1030Z
PRTY:       STANDARD

SNDR:       KOROMO BASE

TRGT:       GHQ

SITREP:     NEGATIVE ENEMY CONTACT FROM
            PATROLS. INTEL RECOMMENDS
            RECON IN SECTORS BB-12 AND
            CB-13. PATROLS FROM
            FIREBASE CHARLIE WILL
            DISEMBARK AT 2300 LOCAL
            TIME.

[END TRANSMISSION]
```

Chapter 2

March 16, 2015

"Thank you Mary," said Charlie as she handed him his 'regular' thirty-two ounce coffee, black and just below boiling in temperature, in a tall Styrofoam cup.

"How's Miss Patricia and the kids? Everybody good?" asked Mary. Mary had worked in the Amalgamated cafeteria longer than anyone could remember. She always remembered your coffee or tea order and had an almost photographic memory when it came to family. If she wasn't the most beloved person at Amalgamated, nobody could tell you who was.

"They're all good, thank you," said Charlie, "Adrian is still over at St. Mary's, Miss Patricia is still downtown at the central library, and the boy Calvin keeps growing."

"He's still growing Charlie? My Lord, you better stop feeding him," laughed Mary.

"Tell me about it. He's already looking me right in the eyes and he's only 18," smiled Charlie, "no telling when he'll stop. Just about eating us out of house and home."

"Is he still looking to get into law school?" asked Mary.

"Sure is," said Charlie, "he's still trying to decide which coast. Stanford out in California or Harvard over in Massachusetts. They've both offered him a full ride, so it's up to him. We've got campus visits set up next month, so we'll see how it goes. I got a feeling that he's gonna be a Cardinal before he's gonna be a Pilgrim. Not too much winter to deal with in the Bay Area. But, we'll see. He might like the 'scenery' better over there, if you know what I mean."

"Oh," scolded Mary, "you'd better not let Miss Patricia hear you talking like that."

"Now who is going to tell Miss Patricia I said that?" asked Charlie, looking conspiratorial.

"Her number one spy certainly will," said a voice behind Charlie. He turned and saw Kelli standing behind him in line with a Cheshire cat grin and a twinkle in her eye.

"Short round," said Charlie, "don't you know it's not nice to sneak up on people and listen in on private conversations?"

"And don't you know, Jolly Green," Kelli began, "that it's also not nice to hold up the coffee line before eight in the morning?"

"Here you are Kelli," said Mary handing her a cup every bit as big as Charlie's. "A Triple, Venti, Half Sweet, Non-Fat, Caramel Macchiato. Shall I assume you're picking up Charlie's too?"

"Of course," laughed Kelli, "this poor guy can barely keep Calvin from starving to death. He certainly can't afford a buck fifty for a coffee." She handed Mary a five and told her to keep the change, as usual.

"You can't really call that thing you drink coffee, you know that, right?" said Charlie.

"Why not," asked Kelli, "it's got coffee in it, plus a whole lot of other yummy things."

"You say so," said Charlie. "You got a few minutes to drop by my office?"

Kelli looked at her watch. "Sure do, I've got about fifteen minutes before the weekly supervisors meeting."

"Ok, good, let's head over to my office."

The incongruous pair walked out the double cafeteria doors to the shop floor and down the main aisle of the shop to Charlie's office. Charlie dutifully held the door for Kelli, who did her best approximation of a curtsey before entering. The walked down the row of desks exchanging good mornings with those of Charlie's staff who were present and into Charlie's office at the back of the room.

Charlie's office was quite spartan, having only a desk with a computer, a four person conference table and an antique coat rack. On Charlie's desk were photos of his wife, Pat, whom everybody called Miss Patricia, his daughter Adrian in her graduation gown from the University of North Carolina's medical program, complete with Summa Cum Laude honor braids, and one of Charlie and his son Calvin somewhere at a lake, with both decked out in fishing gear. Calvin was still a few inches shorter than Charlie in the photo, but the resemblance between father and son was striking.

Kelli dropped down into the nearest conference room table chair and spun it around to face Charlie's desk. Charlie lowered his massive frame into his own chair, which gave the usual squeaks and groans as it absorbed his bulk.

"You need a new chair," said Kelli. "That one's ready for the elephant graveyard. Or it's going to land you on your duff one day when it finally gives up on you."

"Chair's fine," said Charlie as he patted the right arm rest, "just 'cause it's old doesn't mean it's ready for the scrap heap. But thank you for your concern."

"What's on your mind?" asked Kelli.

"I wanted to talk to you about Jack," began Charlie, "because I know you worked with him before. Nothing important, I just wanted to get some background on the guy. I've only interacted with him on the pilot line project so far. I've got a meeting with him later this week to talk about the pilot line and do some target setting for the shop for the rest of the year."

"Ah, so you want the secret scoop on my boss eh?" said Kelli.

"No, nothing like that short round, and you know it," said Charlie, frowning. "I just want to hear something about him so I can better understand where he's coming from. That's all. Don't worry, I'll get to know Mr. Hartmann just fine, but I'd like to hear from somebody who's opinion I respect that has already worked with him."

"Ok, right, so I met Jack about ten years ago, right when I was fresh out of college. My first assignment was to his launch team."

"That was automotive, right?" asked Charlie.

"Yep. It was total chaos. Our program was behind schedule because the program just before ours was a total train wreck and all of the corporate resources got realigned to help fix that launch. So, all of our tools and equipment were delayed as the other team pulled in all of our vendors to try and salvage their own program. Like I said, it was a mess."

"So," said Charlie, "your first assignment fresh out of school was on a launch working for Jack that was already in trouble."

"Exactly. Once we got on-site at the plant and began the installation and trials, things got better, but we were really in a jam. That's when I really began to appreciate having Jack as a boss."

"How so," asked Charlie.

"Well, for starters, he forbade us to attend any launch meetings, and that was great because we could stay back in the shops and get things done."

"Why did he do that?" asked Charlie. "Seems to me that those would be kind of important."

"Not really," said Kelli, "most of the internal meetings were called by the staff launch coordinators. We called them the launch police."

"Ouch," said Charlie making a pained face.

"Trust me," continued Kelli, "if Jack hadn't banned us from those meetings, we never would have built a vehicle, let alone launched. Bureaucracy can be an ugly thing, especially when the pressure's on."

"Ok," said Charlie, "how did the rest of the assignment with Jack go?"

"We managed to hit our final launch date and the plant released us a week after we hit full speed. That had never happened before. My counterparts on other launch teams spent months and months at their plants trying to resolve all of the open issues. We, on the other hand, went home a couple of weeks after full production started. It was pretty cool."

"Sounds like you guys did great," said Charlie.

"Oh, we did, except that's when Jack got himself into quite a bit of hot water with the higher ups."

"Oh," said Charlie, raising an eyebrow. "Tell me what happened."

"It was pretty simple," began Kelli, "all of our parts were delayed because of the prior lousy launch and hadn't been certified yet. The parts have to be run in their home lines at rate to submit for certification. All of our parts were still being made at the tool shops that built them for us. We had to, literally, drive around in a pickup truck after hours picking them up from the different shops just to have enough to build the next day. It was sneaky fun."

"I see," said Charlie, now staring intently at Kelli. "I think I see where this is going, but tell me, how did this get Jack into trouble?"

"We were a week away from a launch gateway review. To pass the gateway, you needed to have eighty percent of your parts certified. We had zero. The higher ups responsible for the launch decided it was time to fudge the numbers and Jack wouldn't go along."

"Why didn't they just delay the gateway review until they had enough certified parts," asked Charlie.

"It was automotive Charlie," said Kelli, "you don't miss a gateway. Ever. The pressure was enormous to make sure the different teams all made it through the gateway and Jack was going to screw that up. The executives would lose bonus and have their careers stalled, if not derailed. They, obviously, would do whatever it took to launch on time."

"And so it played out how?" asked Charlie.

"Jack stuck to his guns and wouldn't fudge the data on his launch status. So, the higher ups just faked the data and didn't invite him to the gateway review. The program made it through that gateway and we went back to work. Eventually our parts got certified and we had a good launch. But it cost Jack."

"Cost him how?"

"It cost him because he got branded a 'loner' and not a 'team player' by the other launch leaders. The executives on launch also had the knives out, since their precious bonus and career was on the line, and they transferred him out of the launch group and into the staff Continuous Improvement group. He never said anything about it. He typically doesn't. He's got this massive stoic streak. Gets it from his grandpa."

"His grandpa?" asked Charlie.

"Yeah, Jack was raised by his grandparents after his mom and dad died in a car crash. Jack was one or two when it happened. A long haul truck driver was into his third straight day, hopped up on speed and trying to make some money, and finally collapsed behind the wheel. The truck swerved, lost control, blew through the median and hit their car head on. Jack's parents were killed instantly and it took the rescue crews two hours to cut Jack's car seat out of the back of the car."

Charlie let out a low whistle and ran his hand over the top of his head. "That's tough Kelli, really tough. So his grandparents raised him from then on, eh?"

"Yeah. His grandpa, Alfred, was a big shooter at Deutsche Bank. From Hannover. Extremely proper. That's where Jack gets it from I think. His grandma, on the other hand, is an absolute hoot," said Kelli smiling.

"How so?" asked Charlie.

"Erika's from Munich. A Bavarian. Trust me, if there were two cultures more in conflict, I'd be surprised. She is every bit as outgoing, gregarious, and funny as Alfred is quiet, reserved, and stoic. She says he was in Munich on business as a young man and she was working the local beer garden. She thought he was handsome and told him so. According to Erika, Alfred turned three shades of red and stammered for a few minutes before Erika was able to get his name. They dated and eventually married. Alfred was working in the Chicago office when Jack's parents died and he and Erika decided to stay in the US and raise Jack. Alfred retired and they raised Jack up in Lincoln Park, north of downtown. He went off to college, got a couple of engineering degrees, to please opa Alfred probably, and ended up working in an automotive OEM. He'd been there about ten years before I met him."

"Got it," said Charlie, "and what about family?"

"Jack's got a younger sister, Rachel, and an adorable niece with another one on the way. Other than that, it's just Jack."

"Are his grandparents still with us," asked Charlie.

"Yep, they're both still in Lincoln Park."

"We should try and get them to come down for the company picnic this summer," said Charlie. "I'd like to meet them. Sounds like quite a pair."

"Oh they are," said Kelli smiling, "Alfred is still trying to get Erika to show 'a little restraint' and Erika is still trying to get Alfred to loosen up. Somebody should make a sitcom out of it."

"So what happened to Jack after that launch? You said he had a fall from grace and got moved around as punishment."

"Oh," said Kelli, "I don't know if it was punishment. But once you get branded like he did, people tend not to give you the benefit of the doubt. He stuck around there another year or so, bouncing from assignment to assignment until he finally left. I had already left and came here. One launch was all it took to convince me that I definitely wasn't a good fit there. Culture stunk. Jack tried to talk me into staying, but there's no way I could have."

"Where'd he go then?" asked Charlie.

"He worked a few different places in Continuous Improvement until I tracked him down one day and convinced him to join us here. He was a bit hesitant at first, but eventually I got him to come out and have a look around. The culture here is nothing like it was when we worked together before. This is a family-owned business and you get a sense that you're part of the family too."

"Old man Flanders, the founder, made sure of that," said Charlie. "He knew everybody by name and never made you feel like you were less than his equal. His son, Zack, who's running the show now, was a bit more of a numbers guy, but he learned from his dad that people don't leave when they're given respect. They've spent their lifetimes building this business and the culture around here."

"I know," said Kelli, "that's why I came here originally and that's why I worked to get Jack here too. Do you think the merger is going to have any effect on the way things are run around here?"

Charlie thought for a minute before answering. "You know kiddo, I hope not, but I guess anything's possible. Amalgamated and Shiloh both put in 45% and the private equity group has the other 10%. The merger teams have been working to consolidate the shared services and I know the supply chain folks have been busy renegotiating our buy stuff, but so far we're not talking about moving any product lines or any facility moves, so I think it's going to be stable here for a bit longer, anyway."

"Well, that's good to hear," said Kelli looking at her watch. "I'd better get going to the meeting. See you later Charlie."

"Ok Kelli, thanks for the talk. See you around."

With that, Kelli picked up her drink and walked out of the Charlie's office, leaving him there with his thoughts about Jack and also about the merger. It would be hard, more like impossible, to undo a lifetime of culture… wouldn't it?

```
TDSTMP:    040315.1200Z
PRTY:      STANDARD

SNDR:      BIG EYE - AERIAL RCN

TRGT:      GHQ

SITREP:    ENEMY FORCE BUILDUP
           DETECTED MULTIPLE
           LOCATIONS NORTH OF FIREBASE
           ALPHA AND EAST OF FIREBASE
           CHARLIE. RECON IN FORCE
           RECOMMENDED IMMEDIATE.

[END TRANSMISSION]
```

Chapter 3

April 3, 2015

The north end conference room was the largest in Amalgamated Industries, seating close to 60 people both around the massive oak table, and two rows deep around the perimeter of the room. There were two tables set up at the east end of the room, draped in white linen, holding an array of coffee, tea, juices, assorted fruits and a dazzling collection of sweets and exotic pastries. The room was starting to fill up in anticipation of the first joint staff meeting between the Amalgamated and Shiloh leadership teams. The merger transition team had been working for months determining how the new organization would function and how the various locations would be managed and more importantly, by whom. Speculation was rampant and as details were 'leaked' they would be immediately superseded by another, more fantastic, 'leak.' After a few weeks of wild speculation everyone realized that there weren't, in fact, any leaks and that all of the sensationalism was simply water cooler talk, albeit on some serious steroids.

"Hey big boss man," said Kelli to Jack, "man, this place is packed to the gills. Amalgamated and Shiloh people. Glad this is a monster room. And did you get a load of that pastry tray back there?"

"I tried not to look too close," Jack replied, cradling his coffee in his ubiquitous Amalgamated coffee mug. Jack had found it in an abandoned supply closet shortly after joining Amalgamated and the mug looked as though it was older than he, having an older corporate color scheme and a number of stress cracks around the handle and base. Jack's team secretly had a bet as to when the mug would finally give up the ghost and break. So far they had been disappointed as the mug soldiered on without complaint, dutifully keeping Jack's coffee steaming hot.

"I know, right? I thought our new health plans were supposed to encourage healthy habits and then they lay out a spread like that. I'm thinking of writing to HR to complain," Kelli said with a grin.

Jack regarded Kelli for a moment and broke into a grin himself, "What did you have?" he finally asked.

"One of those honey-drenched baklava, they are to *die* for," Kelli said with her infectious laugh.

"Have you seen Thanh or Gary?" asked Jack.

"Last I saw them Thanh was trying to get Gary's computer straightened around. A few of us looked at it but couldn't figure out what old Methuselah did to get it so screwed up," Kelli replied.

"I'm sure Thanh can get him back to normal," said Jack, "and I'm glad he's joined our team. That kid is amazingly fast with just about anything I throw at him."

"Yep, he's almost as good as me," said Kelli with a wink.

"And I wouldn't let Gary hear you calling him Methuselah, the world's oldest man," scolded Jack with his best frown and squint combination.

"Your face is going to get stuck like that if you keep doing it boss, and that would *not* be a good thing," laughed Kelli.

'Methuselah' was Gary Phillips, one of the most senior employees at Amalgamated, having joined the company in 1974. Gary had spent his career moving between positions in production, quality, scheduling, and logistics. He was probably the most laid back person you could find, which made him invaluable in the numerous crises that cropped up over the years. He was an inch shy of six feet tall and was a trim 175 pounds. His hair was mostly silver now, having been blonde before that. He joked that it was now 'graveyard blonde.' The left side of Gary's face had a spider web of thin, white scars running from the corner of his mouth out to his ear and coming back ending at his eyebrow, the result of a car accident in his youth, according to him. When he smiled, which was often, deep crags would form near his eyes, giving him an almost malevolent visage. He simply said he needed to get to Hollywood and get the repairs 'done right.'

You would be hard pressed to find a more knowledgeable person about Amalgamated's processes and people, so Jack was extremely grateful to have him as part of his team. Gary had originally planned to retire years ago and travel the world with his wife and childhood sweetheart, Trish, on their 48 foot Beneteau Oceanis sailboat, when a doctor's visit had cruelly changed those plans forever.

Trish, who was loath to spend any time in a doctor's office, preferring to keep an active, healthy lifestyle, began slowing down and having less energy and felt a general malaise slowly enveloping her life. After a few months of this, and mostly due to Gary's insistence, she went to her doctor and had some testing done to determine what she needed to do to get herself back on track. Unfortunately, the cancer that was about to kill her had been growing undetected and had metastasized to just about every major organ in her body. They buried Trish less than a month after the first doctor's visit. Gary's life as he knew it had come crashing down and he quietly imploded, eschewing any offers for help from family, friends, and co-workers and chose instead to find solace in the warming embrace of Scotch whiskey, descending slowly into his own lonely, self-created version of hell.

There were numerous alcohol-fueled incidents that could have cost Gary his job, but the owners of Amalgamated, the Flanders family, quietly intervened on his behalf and allowed him to stay on with the desperate hope that he could find somebody that could help him escape his depression and what was sure to be an alcoholic death sentence. Fate, not friends nor family, intervened one Friday evening when Gary was attempting to drive home from his favorite watering hole, Dooley's, having spent the last few hours performing his daily ritual of drinking himself into a stupor until he just didn't give a damn anymore.

Gary always took an old, seldom used road to get home, the chances of running into another person, especially the local sheriff's deputies, would be remote, at best. He was doing a halfway decent job keeping his pickup truck somewhere between the dashed white line to his left and the solid yellow line to his right. The harsh growl of the rumble strips cut into the road would alert him that he needed to make a minor course correction. His vision was hazy and his reactions were slow when a shape appeared ahead on the right in the ditch. At first Gary thought it was a person standing there, but what in the world would somebody be doing standing there at night in the ditch and dressed all in brown? The deer chose that exact moment to bound onto the roadway and stared directly at Gary's onrushing headlights. Too late Gary realized that he was going to hit the deer and jerked the wheel to the right and slammed on the brakes as hard as he could. The ancient pickup truck, lacking modern anti-lock brakes, began a skid to the right and was heading for the ditch that the deer has so recently bounded out of. Gary's reactions were slow as he cranked the wheel to the left to try and stay on the gravel shoulder, but the pickup refused to obey his commands and only straightened out slightly as it became airborne, hurtling the ten feet over the ditch to the far side where the right side wheels slammed into the side wall of the deep ditch and the truck began an uncontrollable roll into the woods, snapping the saplings like toothpicks, shedding both mirrors and the CB antenna while somehow missing the giant oaks and maples that grew thick there. The truck rolled violently three times, shattering glass and crunching metal before finally coming to rest upright against an oak tree with a trunk easily five feet across. Only Gary's seatbelt had saved his life by keeping him from being ejected during the brutal crash.

The deer watched him for a few seconds before walking to the other side of the road, leaping the width of the ditch easily and vanishing into the woods. Gary watched it vanish into the gloom and began to laugh at his good fortune. He adjusted the cracked rearview mirror to survey the damage and saw that he had survived the crash with only a minor cut above his left eyebrow, which was bleeding into the crags and scars on his face. He stared at his reflection for a long time, an eternity, before years of buried rage exploded from somewhere deep within his soul and he smashed the rearview mirror with his fist, screaming, continuing to hammer at the windshield, hammering at the sick joke that was his life, hammering at the cruel fates that took his beloved Trish, hammering at the hell that was his life. The already shattered windshield yielded to his pounding fist and finally collapsed outward onto the hood as Gary sat there in the driver's seat screaming until his voice shattered with the effort and began sobbing. Everything he had been suppressing, everything he thought he had buried with Trish, came racing back uncontrollably and he collapsed to the ground outside of his destroyed truck and wept, chest heaving, covered in dirt and leaves there on the ground, grabbing for anything that would give him purchase, anything that would let him get up, anything.

He laid there on the ground for a long time until he finally stood, beginning to sober up, and looked around. He saw the amazing beauty and stillness of the forest all around him. He saw the towering oak trees, the ferns that carpeted the forest floor like a soft green blanket, the smaller saplings that were trying to survive on the limited light they received, the bulk being blocked by their taller brethren. Gary looked at his beloved pickup truck, now a shattered hulk of metal and rubber. No body shop would be able to repair the damage he had done. Another loss. Something else he loved was now gone. Gary stared at the truck. He stared and shook his head, reaching up gingerly to see if he had any more cuts on his head.

It was then he noticed his right hand was already badly swollen and his knuckles caked in dried blood from his one-round bout with his rearview mirror and windshield. Broken. In a few places, he thought. Hell, in *all* the places, more like. He stood still, took a deep breath of the musky forest air, straightened up, and began walking back to the road that would take him home. About halfway back to the house that he and Trish had lived in their entire married life a thought washed over him with a warm, comforting embrace. No more. Oh God Trish, I miss you so much. No more…

* * *

"Are you sure you've fixed it?" Gary asked Thanh as the pair walked into the conference room and headed for the coffee and pastry tables.

"Well, I think it's at least usable," said Thanh as he poured himself a cup of tea. "I'm not sure how exactly you could have corrupted so many files on that computer. I've never seen anything like it."

"No idea son, no idea," replied Gary as he grabbed a napkin to go with his coffee and Danish. "Let's grab a seat over by the team. Looks like things are about to get started here." With that they both made their way around the massive table and took seats with Jack and Kelli.

"My name is Veronica Appleton and I am the Vice President of HR for Shiloh," said a thin woman with brunette hair swept back in a bun. Her business suit was by Donna Karan and she had at least 3 karats of diamonds between her earrings and her hands. "This meeting will cover the departmental and personnel changes being instituted as part of the merger," she continued, "First and foremost, there will be no immediate changes in the reporting structure of the operations teams either at Amalgamated or Shiloh. The executive team still needs more time to evaluate the risks and opportunities."

Jack looked over at Charlie, whose face betrayed nothing. Figures, Jack thought, you've got a great leader sitting in this room and we're keeping him on the sidelines while the executive team, who couldn't find the production floor if their lives depended on it, sat in a conference room and debated what was 'best' for the new company.

"Next on the list will be the consolidation of the supporting functions of Quality, Material Handling, Maintenance, Finance, and HR," said Veronica as her eyes swept the room, occasionally stopping to hold the gaze of someone she knew. "For the Quality groups, the labs will remain in place in each facility as will the current organization structure with a change in reporting for the Continuous Improvement groups."

Jack leaned forward in his chair and took a sip of coffee, wondering what this was all about.

"Because the Shiloh CI team has been determined to be more experienced and have a higher level of expertise with regard to the knowledge and usage of the lean tools, the Shiloh team will be designated the lead team and the Amalgamated team will be the supporting team."

Jack felt his face reddening and noticed that Charlie was looking at him with an arched eyebrow as if to ask 'really?'

"Ms. Appleton," Jack said raising his hand.

"Yes?" replied Veronica.

"I'm Jack Hartmann, and I lead the CI team here at Amalgamated. I'm a little confused about how that determination was made. We haven't even met with any of the transition team to talk about what we've been doing here," said Jack.

"Oh," replied Veronica, "so you're Jack Hartmann. Nice to meet you. The decision was very simple actually. The Shiloh team has all undergone extensive online training and certification and are, at a minimum, certified Lean Six Sigma Sensei and there are even a few Master Lean Six Sigma Sensei on the team. Plus, the savings delivered by the Shiloh team is well into the millions of dollars. When we looked into the personnel jackets of the Amalgamated team, we found no such certifications and couldn't find any equivalent number of savings related to your activities here."

"Online certification," said Jack with the hint of a question hanging in the air.

"Yes," replied Veronica with impatience tinging her voice, "it's a very thorough online testing regime where you have to complete timed examinations to demonstrate mastery of the lean tools. I'm not sure exactly what's in the test, but I've been told that it's very difficult and has a very low pass rate. If that's all Mr. Hartmann, I'd like to move on."

Jack forced a smile and sat back in his chair, his mind racing about what this would mean to him and to his team.

"Boss," whispered Kelli as she leaned closer to Jack, "what in the world is she talking about? We looked at that online certification stuff a few years ago and decided it was junk. So you can regurgitate some basics around lean tools, so what? Doesn't mean you can actually do anything with what you know, right?"

"I know," said Jack in as low a voice as possible, "but I guess the transition team valued that more than the work we've been doing out on the floor. We'll have to see what this means, because right now I'm pretty confused."

Veronica continued to outline the changes to the different groups with some consolidating their offices into the Shiloh sites and some at Amalgamated, based on the recommendations of the transition team. The meeting went on for another forty-five minutes until all of the questions had been answered and all of the information had been delivered.

"Thank you all for coming," Veronica's voice boomed over the din of 60 people getting out of their chairs and gathering their belongings, "we'll be sending out a weekly newsletter updating all of you on the progress in each area. If you have any questions, please forward them through your respective HR group."

Jack exited the conference room and walked down the hallway to the double doors that led out to the production floor. The hum of the machinery could be heard through the doors. Kelli followed with Gary and Thanh and the team assembled near the doorway to the stairwell off to the left.

"Jack," began Gary, "I wouldn't take that personally. Those people didn't even bother to come and see how Amalgamated was approaching CI."

"I know, and I'm not," said Jack. "We've done some great things here and have excellent people to work with. I'm quite proud of the work all of you are doing."

"Aw, I'm gonna blush," said Kelli with as sweet a smile as she could muster.

At that moment, Charlie came down the hallway followed by a few of his direct reports heading back to their offices on the other side of the production floor.

"Certifications huh?" boomed Charlie. "Jack, what was all that?"

"There are some organizations that offer online certification. Mostly it tests your book knowledge of the lean tools. We never pursued it because we didn't think it added any value. You learn by doing, not by reading. There isn't a practical component to the certification, just a bunch of timed tests. Or at best there is a barely supervised project."

"Well," continued Charlie, "if you and the gang here are getting penalized for not being certified, maybe you should give it a second look. Don't get me wrong, I like your approach with me and my teams on the floor, but calling you guys the 'support team' seems a bit unfair."

"It's $3,499 per person," said Kelli with a big smile, "you gonna pop for that Jolly Green?"

"Forget I said anything Short Round, forget I said anything." Charlie replied as he walked past the group, clapping Jack on the shoulder as he went and pushing open the heavy doors letting in the cacophony of the shop floor. "Hang in there Jack; keep doing what you're doing."

With that, the doors swung shut leaving Jack and his team alone with their thoughts.

```
TDSTMP:    050115.0530Z
PRTY:      FLASH

SNDR:      KOROMO BASE

TRGT:      GHQ

SITREP:    FIREBASE ALPHA PATROL
           REPORT HEAVY ENEMY CONTACT.
           REQUEST ARTILLERY SUPPORT.
           FIREBASE CHARLIE PATROLS
           ENGAGED. REINFORCEMENTS
           ENROUTE FROM FIREBASE. FULL
           DEFENSIVE POSTURE.
[END TRANSMISSION]
```

Chapter 4

May 1, 2015

Kelli came through the office door in a blur, hanging her coat on the hook designated 'Kelli's, so don't even *think* about it' dropping her purse into her bottom right desk drawer, and tossing her keys into her desk before dropping noisily into her desk chair.

"Good trip to Shiloh Kelli?" asked Gary as he looked up from a Value Stream Map spread out in front of him on the team's conference room table.

"No," said Kelli coldly as she began typing furiously on her keyboard.

Gary stared at her for a while, watching her fingers flying over the keyboard, to the mouse, then back to the keyboard again as she moved effortlessly between tasks. Her jaw was set and she was clenching her teeth hard enough to make a grinding noise. Her brow was wrinkled down the middle and a small vein was beginning to show on her left temple. This, Gary thought, was a look I'd only seen a few times before and it was, thankfully, rare. The kid is upset.

"Kelli," said Gary. No response.

"Kelli," he tried again with a hint of concern in his voice. Still nothing. Kelli seemed to work faster, if that was possible.

"Come on kiddo, it couldn't have been that bad, could it?" asked Gary.

"Fine!" exploded Kelli as she whirled in her chair and was on her feet in the blink of an eye coming right at Gary, who was now retreating behind the conference table with both palms up and facing out toward the onrushing Kelli.

"You want to know how it was Gary?" she began loudly, "it was terrible! We are in big trouble here if that's what we're expected to deliver: or not deliver, or whatever, I don't know."

"Okay, breathe kid, breathe," said Gary in an attempt to mollify his young co-worker. "Tell me what happened for the week you were there; start at the beginning and don't leave anything out, okay?"

Kelli, still wound up and visibly agitated looked at Gary for a long time before her shoulders slumped as she took a very deep breath: Then two. Then she pulled out a conference room chair and sat down. Gary pulled out another chair, although it was safely across the conference room table from Kelli, and sat down.

"What in the world has gotten you so wound up squirt?" asked Gary with concern etched across his face. He enjoyed working with Kelli and had a deep respect for both her quality and quantity of work. Her wit was razor sharp and he did everything he could to teach her everything he knew about Amalgamated. He found her to be an incredibly quick study and always asked questions that were to the point. She was also one of his rare friends, and he hated to see her worked up.

Kelli blurted with a gust of pent-up frustration, "You wouldn't believe the kinds of things they focus on over there."

"Go on," prodded Gary, with an arched eyebrow.

"We focus on problems, right?" asked Kelli rhetorically, "Jack always preaches that. 'What problem are we trying to solve?' he always asks, sometimes until I want to smack him. When I got to Shiloh, I kept asking about what problems they were working on and got completely stone-walled."

"What do you mean?" asked Gary.

"I mean completely stone-walled," responded Kelli with no small hint of exasperation in her voice. "It's like the word 'problem' is radioactive over there. They don't even use it. If they're not hitting a quality number for defects on a product line, instead of calling this a problem, they called it an 'unrealized opportunity,' which is total BS."

Gary thought for a moment then asked, "So they don't like to use negative words like 'problem,' then? That's not unusual these days Kelli, so what is…"

"That's nothing," interrupted Kelli, "compared to how they run their daily business. The morning meetings are something that you have to see to believe. They spend 20 minutes of a 30 minute meeting talking about whether the correct number is 3.251 or 3.3," said Kelli with a slow shake of her head.

"Keep going," said Gary.

"I don't know how to describe it Gary," said Kelli, "it's like they're more interested in being the person that knows the most about a topic instead of contributing to solving the problem. Their entire culture, and don't get me wrong, those people are wicked smart, that culture emphasizes and rewards just knowing more than the other guy."

"How do you mean," asked Gary, now both interested and concerned for what Kelli's week-long trip to Shiloh meant for them back at Amalgamated.

"Take that morning meeting where the argument was over a tenth of a point of productivity. The outcome was the guy that said it was 3.251 was correct and got a big 'atta-boy' from the VP of Manufacturing. Steve something or other. I made the mistake of asking what the number *should* be instead of what the number was."

"And how did that go," asked Gary with a smile, anticipating the answer.

"Like I grew a second head or said that the baby was ugly," said Kelli with a rueful smile. "They all just looked at me for a few seconds like I was speaking Swahili."

Gary was smiling, "And that was it?"

"No, not hardly," continued Kelli, "even the people that just sat down and fired up their laptops to do other things looked at me weird."

"The who?" asked Gary.

"About half of the people in any given meeting are paying zero attention to the meeting and just banging away on their laptops, doing other things," explained Kelli.

"Really," asked Gary incredulously.

"Yep," said Kelli, "so after a day or two I stopped asking questions and just kept my mouth shut and my ears and eyes open."

"That must've just about killed you," said Gary as Kelli stuck her tongue out at him. "So, what other fun facts did you learn about Shiloh's Continuous Improvement activities? Did they do anything worthwhile while you were there?"

"Well," began Kelli, "they did do one of their now famous 'Kaizen Blasts' that they hold up as a global best practice."

"You don't sound impressed," said Gary, "but tell me what happened anyway, so I know it wasn't just your amazingly monstrous sense of pride that blinded you to what others may or may not be doing under the banner of Lean."

Gary was about the only one, besides Charlie, that could talk to Kelli in terms that left nothing unsaid. In truth, Gary was older than Kelli's father and only about a decade younger than her grandfather, so he fit the 'uncle' mold very well. Kelli held a deep respect and fondness for Gary, as he knew so incredibly much about Amalgamated and how it ran, she made a point to pick his brain about something every time they were together, regardless of how outdated or obscure.

"Believe me Gary," Kelli continued, "I was totally pumped to spend a week with their CI team on one of their blitzes, or blasts. Whatever. They've got a very detailed process for what happens weeks in advance in preparation and they have the event mapped out to the hour, including meetings, required data, and checklists."

"Okay," said Gary, "that sounds pretty thorough. No sense wasting people's time in an event when the work can be done offline ahead of time."

"Agreed," replied Kelli, "but that's when things started to go sideways. They always bring in an outside consulting group to run the events. They've been doing it that way for the last twenty years, I learned."

"Hmm, they haven't learned how to run an event themselves?" asked Gary.

"Exactly," said Kelli, "It's like they've had the training wheels on for two decades and still can't ride the bicycle. Weird."

"What about the rest of the event?" asked Gary.

"That's where it gets scary," said Kelli, "For most of the week we just worked as a group coming up with ideas about how to improve the process. We'd put together a matrix and force rank the ideas, and them make cardboard mockups of what we thought was a good idea."

"Okay, I'm still a bit in the dark as to why this has set you off," said Gary.

"Because," said Kelli, "that's basically how the week finished. We made a few cardboard mockups under the direction of the consultants and did some time studies and made signs for how much cycle time we would save or the quality improvements we could make when we implemented the mockups into the line. We had giant sheets of paper hanging all over the place with stick men on them, spaghetti diagrams, you name it. We must've killed a small forest between the wallpaper and the mockups."

"So then what?" asked Gary.

"Then nothing," said Kelli, "that was it. On Friday morning we spent three hours making more wallpaper and rehearsing our report out to the VPs."

"And it was received how," said Gary.

"It was magical," said Kelli with heavy sarcasm waving her arms and staring at the ceiling a few moments before continuing, "all of the VPs; HR, Manufacturing, and Quality all applauded the team's excellent work. It was a giant cheerleading moment with congratulations to all and a deep, meaningful 'thank you' to the outside consultants who led the work. The consultants bowed, Gary, they freaking bowed. They're American and they all bowed deeply like they're monks or something. The team even made a giant 'check' complete with the 'dollars saved' number written on it and gave it to the VP of Manufacturing."

"Seriously, a giant check," asked Gary, now steeply arching both of his eyebrows unconsciously. This was not good.

"Dead serious," said Kelli, "on foam board. A giant check was the only deliverable for this workshop. This was their global best practice."

"But what about all of the work that needed to be done?" asked Gary.

"That the best part. Everything that needed to be done magically had to be done by someone else and it was stuck into a Kaizen Newspaper that covered a four by eight foot sheet of plywood."

"A what?" asked Gary.

"Kaizen Newspaper. It lists all of the tasks that need to be done and has the person responsible's name and a projected due date. But that isn't the best part."

"I'm afraid to ask," said Gary.

"The best part is that it all gets loaded into a corporate database and tracked via their internal e-mail system. If an item is open beyond the due date, the person will get an e-mail informing them that the task has gone beyond the due date."

"Nice use of time," said Gary.

"Oh, it gets better," said Kelli, "Because if you go a full week beyond the due date and don't close out your issue, your boss will start getting copies of the same letters. They call it building 'accountability' into the system. Their HR lady, the one that we met last month here, Veronica, she loves it."

"Robo e-mails to remind you that you need to complete a context-free task item that you may not understand or your boss will get notified," said Gary. "And how does that all work out, did you get a feel for that?"

"I'm glad you asked," said Kelli, "because I went and asked how these giant 'checks' worked through their bottom line deliverables. I spent some time with their Controller and basically found out that the CI activities aren't directly linked to their corporate performance. The Operations groups need to deliver their monthly, quarterly, and yearly objectives as well as support all CI activities. I found a business unit that hit their deliverable of two kaizen events per quarter and chalked up a cool two million in savings. When I looked at the quarter's final numbers, I couldn't find a trace of the two million."

"Uh oh, careful there kid, they might not appreciate that kind of press one bit," cautioned Gary.

"I was careful, don't worry," reassured Kelli, "I just wanted to know what the linkage was and it turns out there wasn't any. That's why I'm not thrilled about this 'global best practice' and what it means for us here. Don't forget, we're the 'supporting team' in all of this." Kelli rubbed her temples trying to make the dull throbbing of an oncoming headache go away. "You're the first person I've told about their events."

"Is that what you were doing just now," asked Gary, "verifying their internal numbers?"

"Bingo," said Kelli, "and what they have, essentially, is a parallel work stream called Continuous Improvement. We're trying to work with the business units here to make sure they hit their targets by focusing on what's important to them, not what's important to us. We can't be successful unless the business units we support with our training and coaching are successful. That's what drives the business units and the entire place forward, right?"

"Okay," said Gary, "Now I know why you're hot about this. There is no way Charlie is going to let us to do that sort of thing out in his operations. Not that we'd even ask, mind you."

"No doubt," said Kelli, "Jolly Green would pop an eyeball and you'd find us all stuffed into the scrap dumpster. If you ever found us at all."

Gary smiled at that, knowing full well Charlie would never stuff Kelli into the dumpster. The rest of the team, he wasn't so sure.

"Well," he said, "You'd better bring Jack up to speed on what you saw and did, because we're about three weeks away from our own Shiloh-led Kaizen Blast out in Business Unit Two."

Kelli's mouth hung open as the thought of replicating Shiloh's process here at Amalgamated sunk in. All of those resources. All of that time. All of the political capital it would require to keep Charlie on board after he saw what the 'new' CI process was. This was going to be a slow motion train wreck.

"You might want to put your poker face back on," said Gary looking out at the shop floor, "because here come Thanh and Jack."

As Kelli composed herself and walked back to her desk, Jack and Thanh walked into the office. Jack saw Kelli at her desk and walked over to her as Thanh headed for the hot water dispenser to refill his mug and drop in a fresh lemon wedge.

"So Kelli," began Jack, smiling, "a warm welcome back to your family at Amalgamated. What did you learn?"

Kelli proceeded to tell Jack and Thanh about her experience at Shiloh, leaving out nothing. Gary came over to join the group and listened to the re-telling of Kelli's week-long trip. After she finished, silence hung in the air as Jack stared at the edge of Kelli's desk. He blinked a few times as he shook himself out of his reverie and looked at Thanh.

"Thanh," asked Jack, "does that pretty well describe the CI work that you were a part of?"

"She has it exactly right," said Thanh looking Jack directly in the eye. Kelli had been working overtime to get Thanh to look at people when he talked to them. He'd been progressing nicely, she thought. His handshake still needed some work, but hey, one thing at a time.

"Everybody at Shiloh," continued Thanh, "is very sharp. You need to be, or somebody will make you look like a fool in a meeting and that would be bad for your career. You spend most of your time preparing for meetings; double-checking numbers; cross-checking facts, that sort of thing. It's a giant game of 'who's smartest?'"

"That," said Gary, "does *not* sound like something we want to replicate here."

"Agreed," said Jack, still staring at the edge of Kelli's desk, his mind racing, "but we don't have much of a choice. We're under a month away from our inaugural event and I've been told that Thanh is going to be our point man for this event."

"What? Why?" asked Kelli.

"To get him," continued Jack, "valuable experience toward his Lean Six Sigma Sensei certification."

"I thought we weren't going to do that on-line stuff Jack," said Gary.

"We," emphasized Jack, "are not. Thanh, as a recent Shiloh CI person, is. They agreed to pick up the cost of tuition for the training and oversee his certification process."

"Well," said Gary, "that's certainly an interesting development. Well done Thanh."

"I smell a rat," said Kelli, squinting now at Thanh, who was deeply blushing and desperately trying to look at his shoes. Anybody's shoes.

"Leave him alone Kelli," said Jack, "This all came from Veronica Appleton. We've got to head down to Charlie's conference room for another get together. She's going to lay everything out and introduce Dean Berzani, who's going to champion Thanh through his certification.

At this Thanh, who was a deep red in color, proceeded to turn to a pale white and look at Jack with a look of mild horror on his face.

"What?" asked Jack.

Thanh didn't speak, but just looked at Jack dumbly, taking shallow breaths.

"Thanh," asked Kelli, "what is it? Do you know this guy?"

Thanh began chewing on his lower lip, unsure as to what to do or say next. He was clearly upset.

"Thanh," said Gary in a low, quiet voice, "you're with family here. Tell us what's got you so spooked."

Thanh looked at Gary and the two locked eyes for a long moment. Gary held his gaze and tried to will him to speak. Thanh then looked at Jack and finally at Kelli, who was smiling at him. He dropped his head, shook it, and then regarded the group while taking a deep breath. Another.

"He isn't a nice person," began Thanh, "but he's Miss Appleton's favorite, so he can pretty much do anything he wants at Shiloh."

"Anything?" asked Gary.

"Yes. In my first few months at Shiloh I had a lot of questions. About everything. The products. The people, the processes. Everything. He wasn't very….. helpful."

"Define *helpful*," said Kelli, still squinting at Thanh.

"He said that if I had so many questions I must not be very smart. He said maybe Shiloh made a mistake in hiring me. Maybe I should go back to China," said Thanh, the look of hurt obvious on his face, "he said that if I wanted to survive at Shiloh I needed to give answers and not ask so many stupid questions. He is not a nice man."

"China?" asked Kelli with a smile, "he doesn't know your family is from Viet Nam? That you were born and raised here?"

"I don't think he cares," replied Thanh.

"Wonderful," began Kelli, "so we've got ourselves an ignorant, racist bigot who's the teacher's pet of our new VP of HR. So what do we do about this guy boss man?"

"We start by remaining professional," said Jack, giving Kelli a hard stare.

"Mafia," added Thanh.

"What?" asked Jack, with equal parts concern and incredulity.

"He likes to act like the movie actor Joe Pesci from the movie Goodfellas. Or perhaps it's the James Caan character from the first Godfather move. You know, the oldest son, Sonny? The one that's always angry and got shot at the turnpike entrance."

Kelli let out a sound somewhere between a bark and a snort as she bent at the waist and clapped both hands on her thighs.

"What?!?" she said as she rolled her eyes at the thought. "Oh God boss, we got us a full-fledged goombah wanna-be coming over to show us how CI is supposed to be done. And," she continued, "he doesn't much care for our guy Thanh, and, the HR harpy is going to feed him to her pet crocodile under the banner of 'development.'"

"Kelli, come on now," said Gary with reproach in his voice.

"Stop. All of you, please just stop," said Jack with sternness in his voice that stopped both Gary and Kelli in mid-sentence. "First, drop the name calling. We don't do that and you know it. Second, nothing is going to happen to Thanh. They've committed to investing some serious dollars in Thanh's certification, whatever we think of it. And more important, he's part of this CI group and we look out for each other. Do you understand that Thanh?" asked Jack, looking at Thanh.'

"Yes, thank you," said Thanh softly. "This has been a very different experience for me, coming here to Amalgamated."

"I'm starting to understand," said Gary, "why you put your hand up for the transfer a few months ago."

Thanh said nothing and simply looked at each of the faces around him and smiled and nodded.

"Ok, good." Said Jack, resuming a normal tone of voice, albeit a bit weary, "let's head to Charlie's conference room and see what's on Veronica's mind and meet one of these 'certified' Master Lean Six Sigma Sensei.

With that the group donned their safety glasses and began the trek across the plant floor to Charlie's conference room. A few minutes later the motion sensor turned off the lights in the office.

```
TDSTMP:    051115.0930Z
PRTY:      FLASH

SNDR:      KOROMO BASE

TRGT:      GHQ

SITREP:    ENEMY CONTACT NEAR KOROMO
           BASE. INFILTRATORS SEEN
           NEAR PERIMETER. PATROLS
           FROM FIREBASES ALPHA,
           BRAVO, AND CHARLIE FALLING
           BACK TO AVOID BEING CUT
           OFF. REQUEST URGENT
           ARTILLERY AND AIR SUPPORT.
[END TRANSMISSION]
```

Chapter 5

May 11, 2015

The team consisting of Jack, Kelli, Thanh and Gary opened the door to Charlie's conference room and saw Veronica Appleton, Shiloh's VP of Human Resources, and another man, presumably Dean Berzani, quietly talking in the corner of the conference room where a coffee service had been set up. Dean was an inch or two shy of six feet with receding brown hair, brown eyes, and a physique that at one time had been toned, but was now trending toward fat. He wore khaki pants with a white collared shirt. Over the shirt he wore a black leather jacket. Veronica was laughing uproariously at something Dean had said when she saw Jack's team enter the room.

"Come in, come in, and sit down," said Veronica as she and Dean sat down, Veronica at the head of the conference room table and Dean immediately to her right. Dean loudly slurped his coffee and leaned back in the conference room chair.

Jack pulled out a chair and sat down. Kelli noticed there was a one chair gap between where Veronica and Dean were sitting and where Jack and his team were sitting. Not good, she thought.

"As you know," began Veronica, "the Shiloh Continuous Improvement team is leading all of the deployment efforts around Lean Six Sigma for both companies. As you'll recall, Jack, you and your team have been designated the *support* team."

"I remember," was all Jack said.

"Good, good," continued Veronica, "and you probably also have heard that Shiloh has graciously offered to improve your team's capability by putting Thanh through the expensive and rigorous training required to be considered a Sig Sigma Lean Sensei."

"Yes, that's very generous of..." began Jack.

"Please don't interrupt Mr. Hartmann," scolded Veronica. That got a bemused smile from Dean Berzani, who was now working over his teeth with a toothpick.

"Now, as I was saying, Shiloh has graciously, and at a financial cost, agreed to invest in your team by having a Lean Six Sigma Sensei trained. It is our hope that he will quickly deliver projects that have a return on investment high enough to pay for his training."

Kelli looked quickly from Veronica to Jack and then to Dean Berzani. She could see Jack's jaw muscles flexing and relaxing as he listened to Veronica. This, Kelli thought, was totally unfair to Jack and incredibly disrespectful to the team here at Amalgamated. And why, Kelli thought, did Veronica continue to talk as though Shiloh and Amalgamated were separate. We just merged, supposedly as equals. And why, for heaven's sake, is she being so rude and patronizing to Jack?

"And," continued Veronica, "to ensure that Thanh's training is both thorough and high quality, I'd like to introduce one of Shiloh's best certified Master Lean Six Sigma Sensei, Mr. Dean Berzani." With that, Dean rocked forward in his chair, stood up and took the toothpick out of his mouth and held it between his index and middle finger.

"Thanks V," began Dean with a thick dialect, "and it's nice to be here with the B team, but call me Sonny," pointing his toothpick at Jack and the rest of the team seated around the conference room table.

Thanh was right, thought Jack, as Dean's mannerisms, including a short breath through his nose, the quick jerk of his head, and the quick shoulder shrugs reminded Jack of a character from central casting playing a local tough guy. Even his thin black leather jacket was probably meant to evoke the 'gangster' look.

"The B team?" asked Kelli, with a little heat in her voice.

"Yeah, well, we need to get youse guys and gals up to speed on how we do things with the upcoming Lean Six Sigma Kaizen Blast event we got in a couple a weeks, isn't that right V?"

Veronica Appleton beamed at Dean as she stood and slowly regarded the group. "You are all so lucky to have a seasoned expert like Dean to get you started in the results-oriented lean six sigma we practice at Shiloh. Please continue Dean." Kelli noticed Jack's neck and ears were now approaching a maroon color.

"Yeah, so here's the deal kids," continued Dean, "we're on track for our event in three weeks. Our external consultants will be here in two weeks to review our preparations and give the go no-go. We've never missed an event and we don't plan to now, capeesh?" asked Dean, as he jabbed his toothpick at Jack and the team. "Our fair-haired boy Van is going to lead the..."

"Thanh," interrupted Jack.

"What?" sneered Dean with a look of distaste on his face.

"His name is Thanh, not Van," said Jack, looking Dean square in the eye. Dean looked at Veronica who had a bemused grin on her face.

"Okay, *Thanh*," said Dean with mock emphasis, "will be leading the event with me as his coach to make sure he don't screw it up too badly." With that Dean and Veronica laughed. When Dean noticed that no-one else was laughing, he continued. "Anyways, like I said, I'll be there to make sure *Thanh*," again with mock emphasis, "learns how to run one of these events."

Gary chimed in, "I thought you said the external consultants were going to be running the event. I'm a little confused here."

"No surprise there pops," said Dean, a bit snidely. "Look, it's real simple; we use the consultants because they're experts. Period. Those guys can walk into an area and in five minutes, bada boom! They can tell you what to do. They've saved us millions."

"If they can do that in five minutes," asked Gary, "then why do we do week long events?"

"Jeez," said Dean, staring up at the ceiling as though everyone in the room except him was a backward child, "We're still learning stuff, pops, until we can come up to their level. I'll run through it again. We been pulling data from your systems so we can understand how the line is running, or how it isn't running, right V?" said Dean as he chuckled and looked to Veronica, who smiled back. "Anyways, we gotta pull all this information together and put it on the standard forms the consultants use. I reckon that'll take us up 'til the consultants come in to judge our work."

"They judge how well we can fill out forms?" asked Gary.

"I think I just said that," said Dean, now with an impatient look, "Once we get the forms all filled out and we get the green light from the consultants, then we get started the following Monday. The first couple of days we'll be assessing the line and identifying waste. I'm sure you guys are familiar with the nine wastes?"

"Nine," said Jack, flatly.

"*Nine*," repeated Dean.

"I thought," said Gary, "that there were seven, maybe eight if you included 'waste of ideas.'"

Dean stared at Veronica, smiled, and then turned, jabbed his toothpick at Gary, and slowly said, "It has been known for years, boys and girls, that the most important waste in any operation is," and here Dean began to slowly say and emphasize each word, "the.... waste... of... missed... opportunities. Did you all get that? Maybe youse should be writin' this down, right V?"

"That's why you're here Dean," said Veronica, "to work with Thanh and the rest of Amalgamated's team. They obviously are far behind Shiloh in their understanding of Six Lean Sigma and will need plenty of training to get them up to some reasonable level of skill."

"So," began Jack, "Thanh's role will be to facilitate the event with the consultants support."

"Now you're catching on, Jackie boy," said Dean. "Thanh will be responsible for leading the event and doin' what the consultants tell him to. And," he continued, "I'll be there to make sure *Thanh*," again with mock emphasis, "don't screw nothin' up too badly, right kid?" Dean was now flashing a wicked smile at Thanh, who was looking right at Dean. Dean continued to stare, expecting Thanh to look away as he always had. When Thanh continued to stare directly at him without blinking, Dean stopped smiling and put the toothpick back into his mouth.

"So, that's it kids," said Dean, talking around the toothpick, "Thanh will be taking his first step to becoming a Six Sigma Lean Sensei. Provided, of course, that he can pass all of the online work, which, is more of a challenge than you might think. But hey, if you fail Thanh, we can always send you a bill for the cost, right?" With this, Dean laughed at his own joke. Veronica made a face and then nodded, as if in agreement. Thanh's face flashed a look of worry.

"Ok," said Veronica, "that's all. Jack, you'll be invited to the report out of the event. You can fill in the rest of the team on what happened and what you learned."

"We typically do things as a team, Miss Appleton," said Jack.

"Yes, I'm sure you do," said Veronica as she stared at Jack through narrowed eyes, "but now you'll do things our way, a *better* way. Your team is not at a sufficient managerial level to warrant their inclusion. *That,* Mr. Hartmann, is why you'll attend and report back to your team *after* the report out. Is that clear enough for you?"

"Perfect, thank you," said Jack, now slowly darkening from deep crimson to purple around the neck.

"We like to keep our meetings short and sweet," said Veronica to nobody in particular in the room, "so I'll let you get back to your duties here at Amalgamated. Thank you Dean, for graciously accepting this assignment. Shiloh will remember your commitment to the team." Dean beamed at Veronica. Jack and his team sat and stared at both Dean and Veronica, mildly stunned at the meeting, or whatever this could rightfully be called.

"You may leave now," said Veronica with arched eyebrows and a dismissive tone.

With that, Jack stood and began walking to the conference room door. The rest of the team got up and followed Jack out the conference room door, leaving Dean and Veronica in the conference room.

* * *

Jack walked into the second floor conference room, his usual haunt, and the motion sensor immediately turned on the lights. He sat down in the nearest chair and looked out the floor-to-ceiling windows at the property that lay to the east. The oaks and maples were beginning to leaf out, now that winter had receded and given way to spring. Jack took a sip of coffee from his battered, cracked, Amalgamated coffee mug. Jack enjoyed little nostalgic reminders like his beloved mug. He knew, though, that his team had a secret pool going as to in what month the mug would finally surrender and break. He just shook his head, smiled at the thought, and took another sip.

He pulled himself from his thoughts as he heard Kelli and Gary arguing about something as they came up the stairwell at the end of the hallway where the conference room was. They came into the room still locked in their argument.

"There are not, you stubborn old goat, *nine* wastes," said Kelli, with heated exasperation in her voice, her hands flailing in the empty air for emphasis.

"Kelli, look," said Gary, obviously trying to mollify his friend, "I'm not saying there are. What I'm saying is that I'm not sure this is a battle you want to fight. You've seen that Shiloh's Continuous Improvement website is full of the nine waste examples. They practically shout it from the rooftops, kid."

"I know, I know," said Kelli in a more even tone, "it's just that it makes me sick how they act like experts and then come up with ridiculous garbage like this."

"I hear ya kid," Gary went on, "but I don't think this particular hill is worth dying on, if you know what I mean."

"Fine, fine," said Kelli, smiling with an exuberance that Jack knew was false, "I'll just swallow this like we seem to be swallowing everything else around here."

Gary was wise enough to end the conversation, even though Kelli was looking at him with half a smile, waiting for the next salvo. Gary knew from experience that this was how his young colleague worked through issues. Best just to let her blow off steam and wait to re-engage when she was in a calmer mood, which usually took about ninety seconds.

"Kelli's right, unfortunately," began Jack. "I want to apologize to you both for what happened in that meeting with Veronica and Mr. Berzani. By the way, where's Thanh?"

"He's right behind us," said Gary, "he was grabbing a fresh cup of tea. I must admit, I was pretty proud of how he handled himself. It had to be hard to listen to Dean. And did you see how those two behaved? My lord, talk about unprofessional."

"I know," answered Jack, "but that's the new reality here. The merger team determined that Shiloh's HR department would integrate Amalgamated's and move a lot of the personnel over to Shiloh."

Thanh walked into the conference room with a steaming cup of tea clasped in both hands. He took a seat next to Kelli, across from Jack. Thanh turned around to look out the windows as he took a sip of tea.

"This is a beautiful spot Jack, I see why you like this conference room," said Thanh.

"Thank you Thanh," said Jack, as he smiled at Gary and Kelli, "because *some* people seem to think it's a little dilapidated and that it should be condemned."

"Only because of the rats," said Kelli.

"Rats?" said Thanh, in a worried voice, looking at Kelli.

"There are *no* rats," said Jack.

"Big ones," added Kelli with a smile.

Thanh squinted at Kelli and then shook his head with a frown. She returned his squint and then laughed.

"Ok," continued Jack, "enough about rats. Even though there aren't any. Thanh, I just apologized to Gary and Kelli about that meeting. There was no call for either one of those people's behavior and I'm sorry that you were treated the way you were. I hope you know that's not how we do things around here."

"I know," said Thanh, "but I told you, that *is* how they do things at Shiloh. Humiliation is considered an acceptable behavior."

"Yeah," said Gary, "I noticed how Veronica seemed to tolerate and even encourage Dean's rather obnoxious attitude."

"Yes," agreed Thanh, "if you can prove that you are the sharpest then you are not held accountable. It is unfortunate."

"I wonder how Carrie is going to get along with them," said Kelli.

Kelli was referring to Carrie Anderson, Amalgamated's current Human Resources manager. Carrie had been instrumental in supporting Jack when he and the team had developed the team member skill matrices for each of the business units. These matrices allowed each of the business units to break down their jobs into fundamental skills that were then taught offline to each of the team members. The effort had begun over a year and a half ago and was yielding significant benefits. The improvements in quality and productivity were immediate and Carrie happily reported to Charlie that year-over-year turnover had dropped significantly in the last eighteen months. The truism that investing in your people increases their loyalty was being born out. The skill matrices were now mandatory, and Charlie energetically supported them, occasionally coming down on his management team if he detected that the people development efforts were slowing or stalled during his weekly reviews.

"I'm not sure," answered Jack, "Carrie certainly isn't hard-wired as a corporate knife-fighter. She likes to collaborate rather than to fight. But I'm sure she'll find a way."

"I hope so," added Gary, "because that woman has been a huge supporter of what we've been doing. When we started focusing on people development along with process improvement, she's been in complete support. Loud support. Which is saying something for Carrie."

"Ok, we'll have to hope for the best for Carrie," said Jack, "but we need to focus on the next couple of weeks to make sure Thanh is ready for the event. Although I'm not sure what else we can do, other than pitch in where you might need us. Just don't hesitate to ask, okay Thanh?"

"Sure," said Thanh smiling, "no problem boss." Thanh's interpersonal skills were improving by the week, thought Jack, who smiled inwardly.

"And," added Kelli, "if you need help with the online stuff, I can be your study-buddy."

"That would be nice, thank you," said Thanh, smiling at Kelli.

"Ok then team," said Jack, "then I think we can get back to work and wash the bitter taste out of our mouths from that meeting. Thanh, you were spot on describing how things are done at Shiloh. If you've got any more insight for any of us, please don't wait for us to ask. I'm not used to defending myself against personal attacks in meetings, so I'd like to pick your brain a bit more." Thanh nodded. "Anybody got anything else?" Jack asked the team. Kelli shook her head. Gary stood up, meaning he had nothing more to add. "Ok then, thanks for coming up here. Let's get back to it."

Kelli leaned over and whispered to Thanh. "And be sure to watch out for the rats."

```
TDSTMP:    052215.1100Z
PRTY:      FLASH

SNDR:      KOROMO BASE

TRGT:      GHQ

SITREP:    FIREBASE CHARLIE PATROL
           TAKING HEAVY CASUALTIES.
           FIREBASE ALPHA TAKING
           INCOMING FIRE AND PATROLS
           ARE CUT OFF. FIREBASE
           BRAVO REPORTS HEAVY ENEMY
           ENGAGEMENT. REINFORCEMENTS
           REQUESTED IMMEDIATE.
           SITUATION SERIOUS.
[END TRANSMISSION]
```

Chapter 6

May 22, 2015

"Thank you Mary," said Charlie as he received his giant, steaming cup of coffee. He extended a dollar bill to Mary but she held her hand up, shook her head, smiled, and looked to the other side of the canteen. Charlie followed her gaze and saw Jack, Gary, Thanh, and Kelli standing in the corner in an impromptu conference. Kelli saw Charlie looking their way and smiled her impish grin and waved briefly before turning back to the conversation with her team. Charlie smiled and shook his head.

"What am I going to do about that child," said Charlie to no-one in particular.

"It's your own fault," offered Mary, "you're the one that takes the bait. I think you enjoy it, matter of fact."

Charlie looked at Mary for a long second and then started softly chuckling. "Yeah, I suppose you're right Mary, short round reminds me of Adrian, my daughter. Except Adrian isn't quite as sassy. They're both smart as a whip and ambitious as the day is long. Kelli will probably be running this place someday. She could probably run my afternoon shift right now."

"Probably so," agreed Mary. "But Charlie, I gotta ask, what's going on today? I see new faces walking around in expensive clothes, followed by a whole bunch of minions dressed just like them, and Suzy, back in the kitchen, tells me she saw a Mercedes and two BMWs out in the parking lot. We got bankers in here for something? I thought we already merged with Shiloh."

"Hmph," Charlie laughed softly, "no, not bankers Mary. Not quite. Consultants. We've got our very first report out on an event led by a bunch of consultants and Shiloh, and our own Thanh, that's him down there; he was tagged with being the facilitator. We're headed out for the final report out in," Charlie checked his watch, "fifteen minutes."

"Oh, good for Thanh," said Mary, "he's such a nice kid. Always says 'please' and 'thank you' and I'm finally starting to get him to smile and look me in the eye when he checks out. Shy one, that Thanh."

"So I've been told," said Charlie, "and yeah, he seems like a smart kid, so I'm interested to see what the final product is out in Business Unit Two. I've kept my nose out of it this week and just let them run wild." Charlie checked his watch again, "And, I'd better get going. See you later Mary."

"Okay Charlie," said Mary, "have a good one."

With that, Charlie left the cafeteria cash register and walked over to join Jack and his team. As he walked up, he saw Kelli looking at him and he tapped his styrofoam cup, closed one eye and frowned at Kelli. She only smiled and winked in response.

"Jack," said Charlie with a nod, "Gary, short round, and the man of the hour, Thanh. You ready for the report out son?"

"Yes sir," said Thanh cautiously. "I guess we are ready."

"You don't sound convincing," said Charlie. "Don't worry son, everybody is nervous the first time they do one of these things. I'm sure you'll be fine."

"Yes sir," was all Thanh said in reply.

"Well Jack, let's get your motley crew here saddled up and head out to the review," said Charlie, putting on his safety glasses.

"We're not going, Jolly Green, only Jack is," said Kelli. Charlie looked at her for a long moment.

"You're not supporting your teammate on his very first report out," asked Charlie, incredulously. "Somebody explain to me, right now, why you've all suddenly lost your minds. Amalgamated is a team. A family. Always was and always will be. I can't believe this Jack, what are you thinking?"

"It's not Jack," offered Gary, "we aren't high enough in the pecking order to warrant going."

"Come again," said Charlie, now completely confused, looking from face to face seeking an answer.

"Veronica Appleton, you know, the VP of HR, told us in no uncertain terms that only manager-level employees and above would be attending the report out," Kelli said.

"You're serious," said Charlie, "where'd *this* idiotic idea come from?"

"Charlie," said Jack, "I've tried all week to convince Veronica and Dean that my team's attending would be good for Thanh and the rest of the team but just kept hitting a brick wall. 'Policy,' she said."

"Well," began Charlie, now agitated, "we'll need to get that policy changed then, won't we. Come on Jack, we gotta go."

With that Charlie pushed open the door hard enough for it to slam against its rubber stopper; the noise loud enough to turn every head in the cafeteria to see what happened. Jack and Thanh simply followed Charlie out to the production floor leaving his team back in the cafeteria to await his briefing after Thanh's report out. The pair had to hustle to keep up with Charlie's long strides as he tended to walk even faster when he was upset. Jack judged that right now, Charlie was somewhere between agitated and explosive.

As they approached the part of the floor designated as Business Unit Two, Thanh broke away and walked over to Dean, who was talking with the external consultants and laughing uproariously about something he just said. Jack saw Veronica Appleton, dressed in what appeared to be an expensive suit standing next to someone Jack had never met. Judging by the look of him, tall, immaculately coiffed very shiny jet black hair, and a perfect smile, this was Steve Bucholtz, the VP of Manufacturing from Shiloh. He was dressed in a tight-fitting crisp blue dress shirt with white collar and cuffs, with the cuffs rolled up enough so Jack could see an enormous watch on his left wrist. He had what appeared to be black, acid-washed jeans with the pant legs turned up revealing what Jack thought, were the most expensive looking shoes he'd ever seen. Hand-made Italian by the looks of them, although Jack couldn't tell. Jack also recognized and nodded to Geoff Mueller, Charlie's business unit leader, Pete Valensky, the area supervisor, and a few others of Charlie's staff.

As Jack returned his gaze to the report out area, he could see a number of movable white boards, which were completely covered in sketches of indeterminate things on both sides. There were also sheets of plywood that had been hastily turned into display boards and around the entire area was a veritable sea of cardboard. Some of it was cut and assembled into shapes that looked vaguely like production equipment, tables, and conveyor belts while the rest of it was lumped into scrap piles scattered around the area. As Jack got closer and inspected each of the displays he recognized spaghetti diagrams, process flow charts, myriad calculations, and what appeared to be a rough work balance chart. He walked to the last board and saw the beginnings of a current state value stream map that had been, by the looks of it, hastily drawn. It was incomplete; basically useless, and Jack looked around futilely for the future state map. A look of confusion and concern began forming on Jack's face. What, he wondered, had they gotten themselves, and more importantly, Thanh, into?

"Ok everybody," boomed Dean to the assembled crowd, "let's get this show on the road. We got some V.I.P.s here and I don't want to waste their time." Dean clapped his hands loudly and motioned everybody to come to where he and the consultants were standing. In less than a minute, everyone had congregated around the display boards, with Veronica and Steve flanking Dean.

"First," began Dean, "I want to thank our consultants for supporting another amazing event." Dean slowly waved his hand to where the knot of consultants was standing. They gave a short bow, which Jack thought was odd since they were all clearly American, with half of them looking like they were fresh out of college. Their matching black suits giving them the appearance of a corporate audit team.

"And," continued Dean, "we'll see how Shiloh's best boy Thanh here ended up doing on his first Kaizen Major Process Re-engineering Blast," with this he pointed at Thanh, who was in front of the middle display board. Thanh smiled and gave a brief wave to the crowd. Jack noticed that Charlie winced briefly at Dean's introduction of Thanh.

"Thank you for coming everyone," said Thanh in a quiet voice.

"Louder," boomed Dean. "We need to hear ya kid, take a deep breath." This got a chuckle from Veronica while Steve Bucholtz simply smiled ruefully and shook his head.

"Sorry," said Thanh, and continued in as loud a voice as he could muster, "we began this week with a complete team here at Amalgamated and I'd like to thank Mr. Charlie Cooks for.."

"Yeah, yeah, skip that kid, we got a schedule to keep," interrupted Dean.

Thanh's face turned a bright pink as he scanned the crowd, now clearly embarrassed. He looked at Charlie, who gave him an imperceptible nod and raised the corner of his mouth slightly as if to say to Thanh, 'you're welcome kid.'

Thanh cleared his throat and continued. "We began with some excellent training from our consultants on a number of things. We learned about the nine wastes, we played a simulation game with children's toys, we did waste identification walks, we did a big session on future visioning and blue sky analysis and idea velocity aggregation." Thanh was gesturing to the display boards and pointing out each of the items as he described them. Jack then understood that the jumble of circles, arrows, stars, and sticky notes was, in fact, an aggregation of high velocity ideas…Or something. A knot began forming in Jack's stomach as Thanh continued his presentation.

"Then, once we were properly trained by our excellent consultants," said Thanh, "they felt we were now capable to go out to the floor, the gemba,"

"The genba Thanh, the *genba*," interrupted Dean, drawing out his pronunciation slowly and loudly. "It's pronounced *GEN – ba*."

"I don't think so Dean, because in the Japanese language the character representing the letter 'n' in English takes on an 'm' sound when it precedes a syllable starting with b, m, or p. So it's pronounced gem-ba even though it's written sometimes as gen-ba."

"What?" said Dean, now obviously embarrassed and looking between Veronica and Steve, head twitching and shoulders shrugging, "so now you're a friggin' language teacher? Keep this movin' kid and don't waste any more time here. These are busy people and the consultants cost an arm and a leg." With this he winked at one of the senior consultants, who only did another brief bow. Veronica was making a 'tsk tsk' sound and Steve just grimaced and shook his head again. Jack looked over to Charlie, whose expressionless face looked like it was carved from granite. Jack looked to Thanh to try and will him to be calm and continue. Thanh was nervously looking down and cleared his throat again.

"Okay, so once the consultants determined that we were ready and trained enough to go to the floor, we began a weighted process flow value analysis of the business unit, taking into account multivariate factors and we then began to capture ideas for the new line design. Once we had force-ranked the ideas into the multi-point exclusion matrix, we were then able to try-storm the potential layout. As we finished the try-storming portion, we then began working on the cardboard cutouts that you see in the area directly behind the display boards." The assembled crowd shuffled forward a little bit to look at the collection of boxes representing equipment, work stations, and conveyors. Jack saw that Steve and Veronica were now having a side conversation at the edge of the group, paying no attention whatsoever to the report out. Thanh let the assembled group look at the mock ups for a few seconds more before continuing.

"Once we finished the mockups and used the virtual production simulation methods that our consultants taught us, we began making the calculations for the expected future state production numbers." With this, Charlie looked over at his production team and specifically at Geoff, who simply raised his eyebrows and shrugged, as if to say 'don't blame me, boss.'

"As you can see here, we expect the line to increase its productivity by close to twenty percent, reducing the headcount required per shift by one operator."

"Thanh," said Charlie, raising his massive arm as though he were in fourth grade and needed to use the restroom, "those cardboard pieces look like new equipment. Am I seeing that right?"

"Yes sir," said Thanh, "those are new pieces of equipment required to statistically operationalize out the future state engineering transformation simulated model."

"You got a cost estimate?" asked Charlie, looking between Geoff and Thanh.

"We unfortunately," continued Thanh, "didn't have time to gather all of those numbers."

"So we don't know," said Charlie, "if this future state is even practical. Or if we have the budget for more capital equipment. Or if this is going to save anything or will actually be a negative to our P&L."

"Hey, don't worry big fella," interjected Dean, "alla that will be worked out in time."

"In time," said Charlie as he turned and looked at Dean, "in time means 'when' exactly?" Charlie's gaze hardened.

"It means probably as soon as your team gets done with the Kaizen list aggregator," said Dean with a smirk on his face.

"Hey Charlie," this from Steve, who had now ended his conversation with Veronica, "why don't we let this report out continue and we can talk about this later."

"Fine," said Charlie, whose features returned to stone. "Sorry Thanh, please continue."

"So, as Dean has said," said Thanh, now with nervousness obvious in his voice, "we have compiled a list of items that need to be completed to deliver this future operational pattern into the web-based Kaizen list aggregator. You can see it here on these last two display boards." Thanh gestured to the final two display boards which held close to eighty items. Each item had a task description, a person responsible, and a required date. Jack could see that many of the names listed in the 'responsible-for' column were not part of the workshop. Many of the items also listed 'TBD' for the required date.

"Excuse me Jack, let me get in there and have a look," said Charlie as he donned a pair of reading glasses and bent down to read the list of items. Charlie looked up and down both boards for nearly a minute before he looked up and turned to Thanh.

"So how does this work," he said, "because what I see here are a whole bunch of task items assigned to people that aren't even here, plus a whole lot of 'TBDs'. A lot of my people and a whole lot of other people. How are we supposed to know how to fit this in with the work we already have in front of us?"

"That's easy," said Dean, "because it's going into everybody's annual performance review courtesy of the Kaizen list aggregator that our consultants graciously let us use. At minimal cost I might add."

"Performance reviews," said Charlie flatly.

"Absolutely," continued Dean, now getting a head of steam up, "we, and by 'we' I mean Thanh, will dump all of this into the software and everybody tagged with a task will get pinged automatically via e-mail if the task goes beyond the due date. If they're late a week, *bada bing*, their boss gets notified. If it goes another week, *boom*, then their boss's boss gets notified until the task either gets done or it ends up in *your* inbox, where the timer starts again. It's simple, do the tasks assigned to you or else the aggregator dumps a report showing who around here's a slug and it dings their bonus. Easy. And brilliant."

"Slugs. Brilliant," said Charlie, staring at Dean with a look of exasperation etching his face.

"It builds accountability into the system Mr. Cooks," said Veronica, "and ensures that the savings are actually realized. I'm sure you can understand the simple concept of accountability."

"Okay guys, enough," this from Steve who was looking at his oversized wristwatch, "Dean, take Charlie through how all of this works offline and let's wrap this up. I've got a flight to catch."

"Now to the good part," said Dean, rubbing his hands together. "Thanh, go get the check for Steve."

Thanh walked around behind one of the display boards and retrieved a two foot by four foot piece of foam board with the likeness of a cashier's check on the front of it, complete with an Amalgamated logo, displaying the name of the event, the date, and the savings that will result. The figure shown was two hundred and fifty thousand dollars.

"Wait a minute," said Charlie, "how did you get that number? Even if we do eliminate two people, which I don't think we can do, that's nowhere near that number. Plus, what if we need to buy that equipment?"

"Very simple," said Veronica, her voice edged with impatience, "we fully fringe the two employees plus we've found that the remaining people work a bit harder after the event, giving us better productivity. Plus, we've factored in the new wage rates the temps are currently being paid at Shiloh. Very simple."

"Temps?" asked Charlie, "what temps?"

"Yes, as part of the integration efforts, the executive board has decided to adopt Shiloh's global best practice of utilizing sixty percent temporary labor, versus keeping all of the old timers around with their inflated salaries and benefit packages. We'll begin the involuntary separations next month."

"My God," thundered Charlie, "you're going to decimate the workforce and somehow think that's a savings? Who in the hell thought this up? And who the *hell* thought it was a good idea?" Veronica took an involuntary step back in the face of an enraged Charlie before she regained her composure.

"Everyone separated, Mr. Cooks, will be given a generous severance package and a financial incentive either for their pension or their 401(k) retirement account, depending on which they have. All of that will be calculated based on years of service."

"Okay, okay," interrupted Steve, "Charlie, you'll be briefed when this becomes official, so calm down and let's keep this professional. Let's get the team photo so I can get out of here. Is the photographer here? Ok, good. Charlie, get in this photo."

Dean took the check from Thanh and held it out in front of him while he shook Steve's hand. Thanh stood to Dean's right and had Charlie next to him. The external consultants stood on the other side of Steve. Veronica came over and moved the consultants so she could stand next to Steve and beamed her best smile at the cameraman. The consultants assumed the position of being in mid-bow while they waited for the picture. The shutter clicked twice and the cameraman looked into the camera's display to see how the photo turned out.

"Hey," he said, "the big guy wasn't smiling. Let's do it again."

"Come on Charlie," prompted Steve through his flashing white teeth, "big smile now, biiiig smile."

Charlie remained stone-faced except to slightly turn up the corners of his mouth, giving him a very strange look, with slightly squinted eyes and a bizarre grin formed. The camera clicked away, capturing the moment for all time.

```
TDSTMP:    052515.0800Z
PRTY:      FLASH

SNDR:      BIG EYE - AERIAL RCN

TRGT:      GHQ

SITREP:    HEAVY DAMAGE SEEN AT
           FIREBASE ALPHA. FIREBASE
           BRAVO OBSCURED BY SMOKE.
           UNABLE TO REACH FIREBASE
           CHARLIE DUE TO HEAVY ENEMY
           FIRE. SITUATION UNKNOWN.

[END TRANSMISSION]
```

Chapter 7

May 25, 2015

Jack was walking down the main production aisle headed for Charlie's office with a steaming mug of fresh coffee, courtesy of Mary in the canteen. He had the weekend to reflect on the prior week's event and what it meant for him and his team, and he was worried. Thanh was back in the office busily typing all of the tasks into the Kaizen list aggregator, which Kelli promptly named HAL, for the villainous computer in the movie 2001: A Space Odyssey.

Even Thanh thought that was funny. Gary only shook his head and muttered under his breath.

Charlie had called Jack over the weekend and asked him to stop by his office first thing after the production start-up meetings were finished. Jack was sure that this wasn't going to be a pleasant meeting as he entered the production offices and greeted those present. He sat down in a chair opposite Charlie's administrative assistant, Taylor Smith, and waited. Charlie's door opened and out walked Taylor carrying a sheaf of papers. She smiled at Jack and sat down at her desk.

"Morning Jack," she said, "how's Monday treating you?"

"I'll let you know after this meeting," Jack replied.

"Yeah, I haven't seen Charlie in this frame of mind in a long time Jack. The production meeting ended a few minutes ago but he's still got Geoff and Pete in there trying to figure out what went on last week. I feel bad for those guys. The bits I heard were that regardless of what Geoff or Pete said, they just got steamrolled by the consultants and the gentleman from Shiloh."

"Dean Berzani," Jack offered.

"Yeah, Dean," continued Taylor, "it sounded like the whole week followed some standard script and no deviations were allowed. Those poor guys," she sighed.

"I got the same feedback from Thanh on Friday when we did our team debriefing. The entire thing was very mechanical and everybody stuck to the script, regardless," said Jack. "Now he's working to load up the database with all of the work tasks. Dean's direction to Thanh was to take all of the 'to be determined' people and make them either the Geoff, Pete, or the other supervisors. Once that gets uploaded, those guys and girls aren't going to be too happy with me or my group. I want to give Charlie a heads up on that too."

"Oh my," said Taylor, "this just keeps getting better and better. Charlie likes you though, so I think you guys can find a way to get through this. Looks like they're coming out."

Seconds later the door to Charlie's office swung open and out walked Geoff followed closely by Pete, looking a bit like the meeting wasn't that much fun.

"Morning Jack," said Geoff as Jack nodded, "can you swing by the B.U. this morning? The earlier the better."

"Sure can Geoff," replied Jack, "I'll come out as soon as I'm done here with Charlie. Morning Pete." Pete nodded at Jack as he walked back through the production offices on his way back out to the floor.

"Thank you," said Geoff, "and be careful in there, Charlie thinks we really got bushwhacked last week and isn't too happy about it. Frankly I agree with him. Last week was totally different from what we've been doing with the pilot line and all I got from it was a truckload of assignments that I don't really understand. That's what I want to talk to you about."

"I know," began Jack, "and the entire team will be there for you Geoff, you know that. Same with Pete. I wasn't sure how the event was going to go, but now that we've gotten one behind us, we can make changes to the agenda."

"Hah," snorted Geoff, "good luck with that. If an item on the agenda was supposed to take two hours, it took two hours, even if we were done in thirty minutes. It's crazy."

"Jack," Charlie's voiced boomed from his office, "if that's you, come on in and let Geoff get back to the floor. If it's not, Geoff, get back out on the floor, you hear?"

"On my way Charlie," said Geoff as he perched his safety glasses on top of his head and headed through the office area to the floor.

Jack got up and Taylor gave him a smile and a wink as he walked into Charlie's office. Jack grabbed one of the four conference room chairs and pulled it over to Charlie's desk.

"Here," began Charlie, tossing a rubber coaster across his desk to Jack, who dutifully put his battered coffee mug on it.

"Thank you," said Jack.

"Where did you ever get that relic," asked Charlie. "I haven't seen that color scheme in, what, twenty years now?"

"It was up in the old second floor east conference room. In the storage closet," answered Jack.

"The one where you hang out, eh? The one with the rats," said Charlie.

"I thought that the rat story was Kelli's idea of a joke," said Jack, confused, "just to mess with Thanh. And us."

"Nope, kid's right. Years ago. They're all gone now. Must've come in with a shipment and they chewed through the walls and got into the kitchen. Main hangout for the things was that conference room until we finally got the exterminator."

"Great," said Jack, looking more closely at his coffee cup and vowing to send it through Mary's industrial dish sanitizer at his first opportunity.

"Jack, I need to know what happened last week," continued Charlie. "I pulled six people, not counting Geoff and Pete, out of operations to support that event. Quality, Materials, and Engineering also supported it. What I expected, mind you, was something similar to what we did over on Line Four. Yes, we pulled some critical people out of their regular jobs to help, but the result was a much better line, and some seriously engaged people. Even Engineering admitted it. Which surprised even me. Plus, Geoff's team was able to drive a lot of the discussion around the re-engineering. Everybody was pulling together to improve the place. We used the productivity improvements to pull out three people and create the new Team Leader jobs, which has led to even better productivity. And quality. And we've got people hassling me asking when their line is going to go through this process. These are all good things Jack, and I'm behind you one hundred percent."

"Thank you Charlie," replied Jack, "we can't do it without your support."

Charlie held up his hand to stop Jack.

"Now listen Jack," continued Charlie, "I said I fully supported what we did on Line Four. What happened last week out in Business Unit Two is a completely different animal. Near as I can tell we spent a week doing a bunch of mumbo-jumbo calculations, making all sorts of pretty graphs and diagrams, burning through cardboard making little mockups of machines and conveyors and then the team claimed a ton of 'savings' but only after everything they listed out gets done," Charlie's voice was rising, "so if I'm expected to accept this, fine, I'll accept it. My team never says the word 'no,' and it won't start now. But you gotta understand Jack, that you, as head of Continuous Improvement, just dumped a whole ton of work on me and my team. Because if I had to guess, I'd bet all of those items with a 'TBD' next to them will end up somewhere in my house. This ain't my first rodeo son, you hear?"

"Charlie, I'm sorry," began Jack but Charlie cut him off, his voice still rising and his face beginning to contort into a mask of anger.

"Jack," thundered Charlie, "up until last week we were on the exact same page. You know I give you and your team everything you need because I know we have the same goals. Up until last week, we've both been working in the same direction; we've both been trying to make this place better. Safer, better quality, better productivity, better morale, everything. But you need to tell me now Jack, if you think you can fix whatever the hell happened last week, because if you can't, then I'm gonna have a really hard time standing next to you on this. You read me?"

"I do Charlie," said Jack, "and we're going to try everything we can to…"

"Don't try, Mr. Hartmann, please *do*," interrupted Charlie, "for all our sakes. This train is headed down the wrong track and if this keeps up, it won't be pretty."

A quick double rap on the door sidelined the conversation as Lyle Whitman, the plant Controller, stuck his head in and handed Charlie two sheets of paper.

"Sorry to interrupt Charlie, but this just came through and you're not going to like it," began Lyle, "I just got off the phone with corporate and they verified the numbers."

Charlie put on his reading glasses and looked up and down the first page, which was their financial report for the first four months of the year along with a forecast for the next eight months.

"Are you kidding," said Charlie to Lyle, "they've already booked the two hundred and fifty grand for that event last week?"

"Afraid so Charlie," said Lyle, "apparently it's the 'new' way we're keeping the Continuous Improvement books here at the Amalgamated site."

"Hold up," said Charlie, "when you say that's the way we're doing it here, what about how they're doing it over at the old Shiloh site?"

"That's the kicker," continued Lyle, "because from what I can tell, we're doing it different than they are. Our stuff goes right into the reports and theirs is kept in a separate account from operations. I asked corporate to clarify and they just said we're the pilot site for this new method."

Charlie shook his head and snorted. "Does Zack know about this," asked Charlie.

"Zack, you mean Zachary Flanders?" asked Lyle.

Zachary Flanders was the son of Amalgamated's founder, Ezekiel Flanders, and was the sole owner of Amalgamated's 45% of the newly merged companies.

"No, I haven't seen Zack since before the merger talks concluded. You don't think he knows?"

"I guarantee it," said Charlie, "no way would Zack let this happen. My guess is the corporate finance deck is stacked against us. Can you bring him up to speed on this?"

"Sure Charlie, happy to," said Lyle, "but I think he's out in Arizona now, just got himself a brand new grandbaby."

"That's right," Charlie said, "his youngest, Susan, I think," Charlie looked up at the ceiling for a second and then looked at his door and boomed "Taylor!"

A voice came back, "I heard, I heard, don't worry Charlie, flowers will be sent before the end of the day."

"Thank you, Taylor, you're the best," he said in response to the open door. "I know," came the reply.

"Charlie," said Lyle, "that wasn't the worst news I'm bringing you. Look at page two where the monthly expenses are itemized. And please don't kill the messenger."

Charlie looked at Lyle with a confused look and then began tracing his finger down the second page Lyle had brought him, which itemized the expenses that were booked against his operations for the month.

"What the…" began Charlie as he squinted at the line item Lyle mentioned, "what is 'personnel development and process improvement support?"

"The consultants," said Lyle.

"What?" thundered Charlie, "are you telling me not only does my budget get slashed by some arbitrary amount because of these clowns but now I get the privilege of *paying* for it?!?"

"Charlie, look," said Lyle, "I spent an hour this morning pleading our case but all I managed to do was get that Berzani guy's salary taken out of the amount and made corporate pick up their travel expenses. Believe me; I tried everything I could think of."

"Thirty grand," said Charlie, still incredulous at the line item staring back from the piece of paper in his massive hand. A piece of paper that was slowly crumpling in a grip that was tightening in Charlie's hand until his knuckles began to turn white.

"Yeah," said Lyle, "two grand a day for the lead guy and a grand a day for the three minions, all of that for six days."

Charlie didn't speak; he simply dropped the paper to his desk and buried his face in his hands. His elbows banged down on his desk and he stayed that way for a few long moments. He looked up, took a deep breath and looked at Jack and then Lyle.

"Thanks Lyle, I know you did what you could," said Charlie, "but see if you can find Zack after he gets back from Arizona and bring him up to speed. I'll also want to meet with you, Engineering, Materials, and the rest to see how this is going to affect us for the year. Right now I'm going to have to figure out how to do some damage control on this. First thing is I'm going to have to drop the Team Leaders out there on line four. Sorry Jack, but there's no way I can cover this hole without starting there."

"But Charlie, all of the improvements-" began Jack.

Charlie held up his hand and gave Jack an apologetic look. "I know Jack, believe me, I know. We'll have to stabilize the line where it is and hopefully we can bring the Team Leaders back when the budget is more favorable. Even then, I'm not going to come close to these numbers. Not without some radical changes in the third and fourth quarters."

"Lyle," said Jack, "can you drain our CI budget for the year to help cover this? We've got some travel funds and some training money set aside. It's not much, but it could help."

"No Jack," interrupted Charlie, "that's not gonna help. Not enough. I need you guys to keep doing what you're doing and help me find a way to get through this. You can start by making sure another one of these *events* doesn't happen again. Clear?"

"Clear," said Jack, although he was obviously unclear how he was going to stand up to the corporate juggernaut of Steve, Veronica, Dean, and their squadron of consultants.

"Thanks Lyle," said Charlie, in a mock happy tone, "you got any more good news or can I go jump off the nearest bridge now?"

"No Charlie," said Lyle chuckling, "that's it. I'll get back to you when I get ahold of Zack. Sorry to be the bearer of bad news. See you later Jack," said Lyle with a brief nod to Jack. Jack gave a tight smile and nodded.

With that, Lyle exited Charlie's office and headed back to his own. Charlie sat there for a moment, looking at the reports Lyle had brought him. Finally, shaking his head, he fed them into his shredder. The shredder dutifully turned the pieces of paper into confetti and went silent. Charlie sat for a few moments alone with his thoughts. Jack thought it wise not to speak until spoken to in this case.

"Jack," Charlie began, "I guess this is the new 'normal' around here. I know this isn't your design, or your fault, these new 'events' that we're doing, but you're the one leading the department, so it's on you. You don't stand a snowball's chance getting that stuff changed, and I know it, so I'm going to need you and your team to go above and beyond yourselves in helping us find a way. All of us. Materials, Engineering, Quality, anything. Wherever we can find savings. I know that's not what we're trying to do, but we can't keep hemorrhaging financially, even if the books *are* being cooked. We clear on that?" Charlie was using his reading glasses to emphasize the point.

"Crystal," Jack said, "crystal clear Charlie."

"Thank you," replied Charlie, "and I'm sorry I got a little wound up. It's been a long time since my back got up that much. I suppose I'll have to go home and tell Miss Patricia and get a scolding. I'll survive," he smiled ruefully and stared at something in the distance for a moment.

Charlie turned in his desk chair and picked up the photograph of him and his wife, Pat, Miss Patricia, on their wedding day. He squinted, then put on his reading glasses, and squinted at the picture again. A look of anger flashed across his face, he grit his teeth, spun around, and looked at Jack, who was now visibly alarmed.

"Charlie, what…" began Jack.

"Jack… Hartmann….," said Charlie slowly, spitting the words, and with malice in his voice, "you tell that sawed-off, sugared-coffee drinking, devious little half-pint that if I can ever find a shred of evidence she masterminded this, she is done for, you hear me, *done for*!!" Charlie's hand slapped down on his desk like a thunderclap.

"But Charlie, I don't…" stammered Jack.

"Here," boomed Charlie as he shoved the photograph at Jack. Jack looked at it closely and couldn't see anything amiss until he looked at Charlie's face in the photo. The original photo had a young Charlie smiling back at the camera as he held onto his new bride's hands; a more perfect definition of joy couldn't be found. As jack looked closer at the photo, he could see that somebody had taken a copy of the recent 'check presenting photo,' taken after the Kaizen Blast event, complete with Charlie's bizarre smile, and cut it out and placed it over his face in the picture.

"Oh my. Oh no," said Jack, "Charlie I…"

"Aw no, no, no, no," said Charlie shaking his head, "she got all my photos. Jeez, short round got 'em all."

Jack looked at the other photos on Charlie's desk and saw that each one had the same 'smile' picture, sized perfectly, and placed over Charlie's face. The time and effort it took, not to mention getting into Charlie's locked office over the weekend, had all the hallmarks of his resident prankster, Kelli O'Malley. And Charlie knew it. Jack looked at the other photos and then at Charlie, who was still shaking his head. Finally a smile broke across Charlie's face and he turned to Jack.

"Out, Mr. Hartmann, get *out* of my office. Now." said Charlie, amused at the audacity of this prank, "and you tell short round that I'm dusting for prints in here. I'm calling in the local police and the FBI. And tracking dogs. I'm getting some tracking dogs. And you make dang sure she knows that she just made number *one* on my number *two* list, if you get my meaning," this to Jack's retreating back as he headed for the door as fast as he could walk without actually breaking into a jog.

As Jack walked past Taylor's desk he noticed she had both hands over her mouth, desperately trying not to laugh out loud. Jack thought he might have identified a co-conspirator. Never a dull moment around here; I'll have to thank Kelli right before I strangle her, thought Jack, smiling inwardly at her joke. His smile didn't last long, as thoughts of the recent event, the financial penalties that had been levied against Charlie and his team, the rather corrosive clash of personalities with the Shiloh team, and the impending demand to hold even more events. A dull ache began to form at Jack's temples and he began to rub them as he walked back to his office to share the news with the rest of the team. This isn't going well….

```
TDSTMP:    062215.1300Z
PRTY:      URGENT

SNDR:      KOROMO BASE

TRGT:      GHQ

SITREP:    FIREBASE ALPHA ABANDONED.
           FIREBASE BRAVO UNDER HEAVY
           ASSAULT. REMAINING TROOPS
           ORDERED BACK TO KOROMO
           BASE. MASSIVE EXPLOSIONS
           SEEN IN VICINITY OF
           FIREBASE CHARLIE. ALL
           COMMUNICATION LOST.

[END TRANSMISSION]
```

Chapter 8

June 22, 2015

It had been a month since the first Kaizen Major Process Re-engineering Blast, and the fallout continued. The matrix that Thanh had filled out and uploaded to the internal website was dutifully sending out e-mails notifying people that they had not completed their tasks during the allotted time. Numerous e-mails were now flying up and down the organization trying to reprioritize work to absorb the tasks from the Blast.

A second shockwave rippled through Charlie's organization as the 'escalation' emails started going out. Now supervisors had to respond to their manager when tasks got 'elevated.' The escalation process continued until Charlie's inbox began to fill up with task after task. He and his staff began holding weekly meetings to try and sift through the items and see what made sense and what was just gibberish. After two weeks of digesting the workload, Charlie invited Jack and Thanh to his meeting to help decipher some of the remaining open items.

"Morning Charlie," said Jack as he walked into the conference room, followed by Thanh.

"Gentlemen," replied Charlie in greeting as he turned from his chair to look at the newcomers, "please get some coffee over there, this is going to take a while I'd guess."

Jack and Thanh walked to the conference table set against the wall and each grabbed a styrofoam cup and filled it; Jack's with black coffee and Thanh's with hot water to which he added an English breakfast teabag. The pair walked back to the conference room table and sat down. Jack sat opposite Charlie and Thanh next to Geoff Mueller.

"Ok, first, thanks for coming," began Charlie, "I appreciate the help."

"Of course," said Jack, "we're glad to help. We're the ones that helped create this mess, so we'd better be in on the fixes."

"True, Mr. Hartmann," from Charlie, "very true. I just didn't want to hold that over your head. Now, we've gotten through most of the items that made sense to us, but we've got a bunch left that we can't make heads or tails out of. That's why we called you in."

"Okay, shoot," said Jack, "what's the first one?"

Charlie pulled his reading glasses out of his shop coat pocket and put them on the end of his nose as he began to read down the list. "Ok, here's the first one Jack, Item 36 says that we need to complete a 'material cost/mass velocity flow analysis for any available conveyance pathway for eighty percent of the salable value of the end product. You got any idea what that is, 'cause we sure don't."

Jack looked at Thanh and raised his eyebrows. Thanh looked nervously around the room and cleared his throat.

"Yes, the consultants explained that to us during the training week," began Thanh.

"Consultants huh," snorted Charlie, "why do I think this is going to be something that won't make me happy. At all."

"The material cost/mass velocity flow analysis is a study to determine the usage of conveyance pathways, aisles and the like, to determine if the line is part of an optimally flowing worksite," offered Thanh.

"Come again," said Charlie, with a look mixed with amusement and confusion. "Now please tell me why, young Thanh, would I ever want to spend time doing something like that?"

"Um," said Thanh, looking at the table as he gathered his thoughts, "why don't I just take that one. Dean had me assign it to Geoff and his team, but I don't think they should spend time working on it."

"Why?" asked Charlie.

"Because," continued Thanh, "it probably won't give us any useful information about the line. We had to do it as part of the standard Blast methodology that we learned from the consultants. Nobody really understood what it was, but we still had to do it, or at least put it into the list aggregator. I can run the analysis and keep the Shiloh folks happy."

"See boss," said Geoff, "I *told* you we got railroaded into doing a bunch of garbage that nobody could understand. The consultants basically made it seem like we weren't smart enough to understand their 'proprietary methods of analysis.' We just kept our mouths shut."

"Excellent, Geoffrey, I'm pleased to hear that" said Charlie, "'cause that's how you learn. But the problem now is that we have this task and whole bunch of others that we need to get closed out in this new *system*," Charlie emphasized the word 'system' for effect, "and just about all of them are now assigned to me."

"We'll take it from here," said Jack, scanning the list of open items. "I have no idea what some of these things are, but we'll get to the bottom of it and if we need your help, we'll circle back. How about that?"

"Sounds fine Mr. Hartmann," said Charlie, "but I need you to do one more thing for me as well, about this aggregator whatever it is."

"Sure," said Jack, "name it."

"This wonderful new system, once it bumps a task up the chain of command, also creates a report that goes to the HR e-mail basically stating that the person who couldn't complete the task on time has 'failed in their basic job duties.'"

"It what?" exclaimed Jack, both amazed and terrified. "Why does it do that?!?"

"Your buddy Dean, remember," continued Charlie, "it is, how did he put it, ah yes, it is *simple* and *brilliant*. Now I've got a shop full of hard-working people that are getting rat notes sent to HR about not completing tasks that nobody understands, including you, right?"

"I guess so," began Jack.

"Guess nothing, Mr. Hartmann," said Charlie, now giving Jack a hard look, "you said you were going to make this right, and this is what I need done. Understand?"

"Understood Charlie," said Jack, "I'll take care of it."

"Good," said Charlie, "then I guess this won't take very long after all. Thanh, you run down that list and grab whoever you need from here and get those things done. Jack, you make sure those e-mail rat notes don't end up in anybody's permanent file. Call it a *pilot*. Whatever. I don't care. Just make sure nobody gets dinged, clear?"

"Very clear," said Jack, who was not remotely clear on how he was going to be able to pull this one off. He'd need the help of Carrie Anderson, in HR, on this one.

"Good," said Charlie, "then take your free coffee and get out of my conference room. We got real work to get done here." Charlie was smiling now as he pointed to the conference room door.

"Thanks Charlie," from Jack as he and Thanh got up to leave, "we'll circle back in a few days."

Jack and Thanh walked out of the conference room back through the production offices and out onto the floor. Jack stopped in the pedestrian aisle and pulled out his cell phone.

"Who are you calling," asked Thanh.

"Texting Kelli and Gary," said Jack in reply, "I want to head over to Carrie's office and see what we can do about these automated e-mails."

"Oh," said Thanh, "that's good. She'll have to do something manually in their system though, because those e-mails are hard-coded to go right into each person's electronic file that HR keeps."

"You're kidding," said Jack, looking at Thanh with a look of exasperation on his face. His temples were beginning to throb when his phone buzzed, alerting him of an incoming text. He looked at it and furrowed his brow at Kelli's response.

"What is it," asked Thanh.

"Kelli says only that 'I obviously haven't heard, see you when you get here." Jack looked at the message again and dropped his phone back into his pocket. He and Thanh set off up the main aisle to the front offices to see if they could get some clarity from Carrie as to what, exactly, was going on.

The walk took less than two minutes and Jack, followed by Thanh, swung open the big double doors that led to the front office area. They both put their safety glasses on the tops of their heads as they walked down the hallway past finance, logistics, quality, engineering, and finally reached the HR area.

Jack could see Carrie's office door was open and could hear Kelli talking to Gary. As he walked through the doorway, two things struck him. First, Carrie's nameplate was missing from the door and more shocking was the fact that her office was completely empty, except for a machine that resembled an ATM sitting in the middle of her office. Jack looked around the rest of her office and saw no traces of Carrie. Everything had been removed and the strange new kiosk had been installed. There was still concrete dust around the bolts used to secure it to the floor. Jack could see where the concrete floor had been cut to install the communication cable from the wall jack over to the kiosk.

"What," began Jack, "where is…."

"Corporate," explained Kelli with resignation in her voice.

"When?"

"Friday afternoon. She got an e-mail telling her that effective immediately, her office was now over at the corporate HR office, at Shiloh's facility."

"I'd like to introduce," said Gary, with his arm draped over the top of the kiosk, "our new HR representative." He slapped his open palm on the top of the kiosk twice, as if patting a dog.

"You're kidding," said Jack, incredulously.

"Nope," said Kelli, "this is, apparently, part of the merger team's plan to find synergies, or whatever. Nice, eh?"

"No," said Jack flatly.

"Here," said Gary, "I'll show you." He walked around to the front of the kiosk, bent down, and put his face close to the screen. "HAL, open the pod bay door."

Thanh and Kelli laughed. Jack simply looked at Gary, who was smiling at his own joke.

"Don't tell me Jack," said Gary, noticing the confused look on Jack's face, "you're not a big science fiction fan?"

"No, not really," replied Jack.

"2001: A Space Odyssey? HAL9001?"

Jack just shrugged at Gary with his palms facing upward. Kelli was making a tut-tutting sound and even Thanh was smiling.

"Ok boss," offered Kelli as she popped a lollipop into her mouth, "I'll make it simple. HAL was the computer that ran the ship in the movie. It was evil and was trying to kill the crew. They had to kill it to survive. End of story. Meet HAL." Kelli swept both of her hands from her sides to the display screen on the kiosk.

"I thought the aggregator was HAL," said Jack.

"Not anymore," said Kelli, "this thing is way worse."

"So, if I understand this, you all think that this new HR kiosk is going to try to kill us then, is that it?" asked Jack.

"Not at first," replied Kelli.

"First it will act like our friend," added Thanh, smiling.

"Exactly," said Kelli, popping the lollipop out of her mouth and pointing it at Thanh. "This thing will try and be our friend and when we're all lulled into a false sense of security, BAM, it tries to kill us. I think Gary's a goner for sure…"

"Watch it squirt," said Gary, "I'm old but I've still got a trick or two up my sleeve."

"Polyester sleeve, you mean" said Kelli laughing.

"Ok, enough," interrupted Jack, "what does this mean in the bigger picture here?"

"Well," answered Gary, "this kiosk is loaded with lots of data on policies, payroll, retirement, you name it. You just come in here, pop in either your social security number or your employee number and ask away. If it doesn't have the answer you need, it prints out a little slip of paper with the phone number on it that you can call to get what you need."

"Phone number," said Jack.

"Yep. We now have an outside third-party service handling all of the basic HR needs of the company. I think they're in India, or Thailand, or some such place. We still have a few of the managers, like Carrie, over at their main office at Shiloh for anything the kiosks and telephone people can't handle. Anything we used to go to Carrie for we now get from this little bit of technology here," said Gary, patting the side of the machine.

"Does it do," asked Kelli, "the worker cross-training and skill matrices like Carrie used help us with?"

"Um," said Gary, "good question, let me ask." With that he turned and began typing on the keyboard located below the screen. After a moment he hit the 'enter' key with a flourish and waited for a response. The group waited and watched as Gary leaned closer to the screen, squinted, tilted his head to the left and then the right. He finally began to slowly stroke his chin as he looked at the screen. After a moment he stood up, turned, and addressed the group.

"No."

"Well duh," said Kelli, "I could have guessed that."

"But I do have a phone number that we can call and find out more information," added Gary.

"Forget it," said Jack, "this is something else we're going to have to figure out how to deal with. Carrie was, as you all know, instrumental in getting those skills matrices set up and running smoothly. Charlie and his team loves them, the teams like them because it gives them a snapshot of where they are and where they're trying to get to, and it was helpful for Carrie to see how each area was coming with their People Development activities. With our HR group here now effectively outsourced to this," he paused and regarded the silent kiosk, "this *thing*, we're going to need a Plan B. I'm not sure this day can get much better." Jack closed his eyes and began lightly rubbing his temples. What had started as a dull throb was now turning into a stampeding herd of angry, over-caffeinated elephants on pogo sticks.

"Jack," began Thanh, "I didn't want to say anything in front of Charlie."

"What?" asked Jack as he stopped rubbing his temples and stared at Thanh. "Tell me this isn't more bad news."

"I'm sorry Jack," continued Thanh, "but you know how we took on the assignment to finish all of the tasks from the Kaizen Major Process Re-engineering Blast that Charlie didn't understand?"

"You mean all of the *'lean phrenology'* work," added Kelli, disdain obvious in her voice. This got a smile from Gary and an exasperated look from Jack.

"Yes," said Thanh. "Anyway, in order to complete those tasks we need to use the software and links that Dean Berzani provided after the event."

"Yes, I know all that Thanh," said Jack.

"But," continued Thanh, "did you also know that we are simply using the consultants' software and servers?"

"No," said Jack, "I didn't. You mean that software isn't ours?"

"No," answered Thanh, "we rent it from them. Each time I access a different program to do one of the tasks, we will get charged a fee. If I need to log in multiple times, we will get multiple charges for the same task."

Jack let out a deep breath through his nose, closed his eyes, and began massaging his temples again, wondering if it were anywhere near time to go home for the night. Unfortunately, it was almost ten o'clock in the morning.

"Let me get this straight," said Kelli, talking around the lollipop in her mouth, "they've created some proprietary software to do a bunch of garbage calculations," now the lollipop was out and being used as a pointer, "that mean nothing to the operation, they load up one of their events with assignments that *require* you to use this software, and then *charge* you to use it. Un-freaking believable." Kelli was stalking around the room waving her lollipop for effect.

"They also," added Thanh, "charged us for the forms that we used. The ones with the Japanese writing all over them. I checked with Lyle Whitman and he confirmed it in the detailed invoice."

"Nice business model," added Gary. "Plus, Jack, you also told us that the bill for the event hit Charlie's expense account and his budget for the year got clipped for the 'savings' generated in the event. We're getting pressure from 'Benito' Berzani to do another event, which will get you promptly killed by Charlie so I don't recommend it, and now we've just lost our HR support. People Development effectively died last Friday afternoon."

"I know, I know," said Jack, still rubbing his temples, in a weary voice, "just slow down everybody. We need to figure this out. Everything we've worked so hard for is getting pulled apart. We've lost our Team Leaders out on line four, the best of the workforce who helped us eliminate their jobs so they could *become* team leaders, we're chasing our tails on assignments that mean nothing and cost real money, we just lost our HR support, and we're getting pressure to do it again from our senior leadership over at Shiloh and their Continuous Improvement group."

"That's a nice summation Jack," offered Gary.

Thanh chimed in, "We must make sure we get the tasks done correctly the first time to minimize cost."

"Or," said Kelli, "we can just pencil whip the assignment and sign off on it on the on-line system and save the money. We wouldn't use whatever reports came out of that software anyway, so why should we waste the time or money?"

"You're advocating we lie?" asked Gary, eyebrows raised.

"Not lie, no" said Kelli, "just not be *exactly* forthcoming with everything we do to get the final tasks for the event closed--- yes, alright, fine, we lie. Boldly. Shamelessly. Who's with me?" Kelli looked from face to face with a wicked smile on her face.

"No," said Jack, "we do it by the book. But we're going to have to find a way to keep the pilot line supported as well as the Kaizen event area in Business Unit Two."

"That's a tall order Jack," said Gary, "as we're already short-handed out on the floor. I don't know. I just don't know. We're getting killed here."

No-one had an answer for Gary and the group stood silently in Carrie Anderson's old office. The kiosk beeped once and the screen went dark as it went into 'sleep' mode.

'Et tu Brute?' thought Jack to himself, looking at the now silent machine.

```
TDSTMP:      072115.0530Z
PRTY:        EMERGENCY

SNDR:        KOROMO BASE

TRGT:        GHQ

SITREP:      SITUATION DESPERATE. ALL
             FINAL FIGHTING POSITIONS
             MANNED AT KOROMO. ENEMY IS
             MASSING ON ALL SIDES. HEAVY
             CASUALTIES. AMMUNITION
             STATUS LOW. REQUEST
             IMMEDIATE REINFORCEMENTS OR
             KOROMO WILL FALL.

[END TRANSMISSION]
```

Chapter 9

July 21, 2015

Gary was standing in front of the production control board for line four, the original pilot line, looking at the line performance over the last few months. The high level indicators for Safety, Quality, Cost, and Delivery were all moving toward their targets, but it was obvious to anyone who could see, that the improvements had begun to level off.

What Gary and everyone else knew was that when Charlie had to put the team leaders back into the department as team members, the first line of support for the lines had effectively vanished. No longer would the team leaders be able to answer the calls for help via the Andon system that was now in place. Now it was the supervisor's job to ensure the smooth flow of production. Quality problems weren't being systemically addressed as they had been. Now, rather, the organization was focused on attacking any issue that either stopped production or directly impacted the customer.

Amalgamated was beginning to focus on the utility of a few people to jump from fire to fire and quickly apply whatever was needed to get the lines running again or to mollify an upset customer. Gary had seen this before in his almost four decades with Amalgamated. Business would be good and the money flowed for improvement projects, training, and any other internal investment you could imagine. Then, inevitably, when the business outlook soured, the inevitable cuts would come. First travel budgets would get 'frozen,' followed by the elimination of non-essential, which meant anything not mandated by law, like training, followed by an increased scrutiny over any expense, no matter how trivial. It would take a manager's approval to buy a case of toilet paper for the restrooms. Ebbs and flows, Gary thought to himself, ebbs and flows.

This time, though, things were feeling a bit different, and not in a good way. Maybe it was the merger. Maybe it was the impact of the two wildly different cultures that existed at Amalgamated and Shiloh. Differences that would never show up on a spreadsheet or an analysis or whatever the quants used when they decided to merge the two companies. God bless the bean counters, Gary thought, no matter how bad things got there never seemed to be any reductions in that area. He smiled to himself and refocused on the production control board. What, he wondered, are we going to be able to do to turn this ship around?

"Stuck on a word," asked Kelli, walking up behind Gary, "sound it out, maybe I can help."

"No, squirt," said Gary, laughing, "I'm not stuck on a word. Man, you really don't have an off switch do you?"

"Nope," said Kelli smiling, "full speed ahead and damn the torpedoes. Only way to live."

"I assume *that* particular logic is why you took it upon yourself to bring that set of lawn darts to the company picnic this year, right?"

The annual company picnic, held two weekends ago, was one of the highlight events at Amalgamated, second in popularity only to the Christmas party. Unless someone was away on vacation or ill in the hospital, they and their families were at the company get-togethers. This year Kelli had surprised the gathering by producing an ancient set of lawn darts and an impromptu tournament quickly started. Brackets were created and the contestants battled all afternoon until finally the last game came down to Kelli and her partner, Pat Cooks, Miss Patricia, versus Tom Donaldson, the Engineering manager and Susan Larkin, the Logistics manager. The battle raged back and forth, with one team falling behind and then catching back up. Neither team could pull ahead far enough to win so the score kept ratcheting up well beyond the twenty one points needed to win. Side bets began to be made as the crowd grew. Shouts of joy would go up when Miss Patricia dropped a lawn dart cleanly in the circle to be followed by chants of SU-SAN SU-SAN when she matched Pat's accuracy on her next throw, her dart landing almost on top of Pat's. The game finally ended when Tom's throw came down just outside the ring and Kelli's next throw was a perfect bullseye. The crowd let out a roar and hugs were exchanged all around amongst the combatants. Bets were paid and challenges were issued for next year's picnic.

"Lawn darts," began Kelli, "are a *lot* more fun than throwing stupid beanbags at a piece of plywood. Corn hole. Great name. What moron invented that?"

"Lawn darts, kid," said Gary, "are dangerous."

"Only," corrected Kelli, "if you're an idiot. Notice not one person ended up in the emergency room. My God Gary, should we all wear sumo suits, helmets, and mouth guards? Maybe we should never go outside because we might get hurt. Maybe we shouldn't drive cars because people die on the roads every year. Maybe we should ban every potential activity where people might get hurt if they don't use the common sense God gave a chair."

"But Kelli," began Gary.

"But nothing," continued Kelli, now with a head of steam up. "Why don't we just let some faceless bureaucracy somewhere tell us how to live every aspect of our lives? You know, *for our own good.*"

"Is that what's got you peeved today," asked Gary, "the fact that we seem to be losing the battle against a faceless bureaucracy here?"

"No," said Kelli, brow furrowed, "yes. I don't know. What's happening here is a *crime*. We're cutting out muscle tissue Gary, not fat. All in the quest to pump up our financials so if and when we go public, the genius executives will get a higher price for their options. If I hear the phrase 'best practice ratio of blah blah blah again, I'm going to puke!"

"Okay Kelli, okay," said Gary, hands up defensively, "I hear you. I must admit, though, the company picnic was fun, and I even made twenty bucks betting on you and Pat."

"You're smart, for a fossil, and you're welcome," said Kelli now smiling slightly, "now, what's got you so interested here on the production control board?"

"I'm just looking at the trends for the year. We started out reasonably well and you can see where we dipped a bit back when we did the pilot line initial work, but then it really took off after that."

Kelli looked at the charts for a moment and then regarded Gary. "Entropy," she said, looking at him evenly, "entropy is starting to kick in."

"Say again," prompted Gary.

"Entropy, decay, is eating away at our system, driving the performance in the wrong direction. We're not putting any more energy into the system, so it's starting to unwind. Backsliding, Gary," continued Kelli, "that's what you're looking at isn't, it?"

"No, not really, at least not yet" said Gary, looking back at the board, "we're not backsliding yet but we're starting to flat-line on a lot of things. Look here at the rework numbers," Gary's finger traced the line from its January high down to May where it started to flatten out, "you can see that we've been trending down, in a bumpy way, but the trend is still down until here. We start to flatten out here in Mid-May."

"When we pulled out the team leaders," said Kelli.

"Right. When we pulled out the team leaders. Now we don't have anybody to work with the teams to drive problem solving. We used to find a problem and immediately walk the line until we identified what we thought was the root cause, countermeasured it, and then monitored for recurrence. Now, the teams are doing their best, but they don't have the time to do anything other than find, fix, and repair. Simple containment only. To make matters worse, now we've got all of these 'lean audits' that we need to get done to report up to corporate CI."

"I know," said Kelli, "Thanh and I are trying to automate these things as best we can, but there's a lot of paper being generated."

Since the May event, new audit requirements have been popping up all over Amalgamated's operations. There are now audits to record the status of 5S, stock levels, machine conditions, waste walk reports, and a recent report showing the number of suggestions submitted by each team member. The results of the audits are tallied and then plotted on eleven by seventeen inch paper in full color showing the progress of the particular metric to its target. The 5S audit report, for example, has a ten point grading scale for each area audited plotted as a ten-period exponentially smoothed moving average. Line four's current 5S score was averaging six point four, with the year's target marked with a red line on the chart at seven point three. Below the colorful chart was a list of actions the teams were taking to close the gap. Most of the tasks listed showed that the responsibility was listed as 'team' and the due by date was shown as 'ongoing.'

"Automating these things has gone a long way," said Gary, "in getting the floor to use them. I know the teams appreciate what you two are doing."

"Glad to be appreciated," said Kelli, "I just wish we could spend more time on critical things instead of this administration junk."

"I know Kelli, me too, but we've got to do this or corporate will come down on Charlie, and us too, for that matter."

"Gary," asked Kelli, "how long do you think we're going to have to keep this up? This stuff has absolutely nothing to do with supporting lean transformation. We're running around measuring a bunch of meaningless things, spending time and money to make pretty charts, and then holding people 'accountable' to move the numbers. We demand suggestions from the teams and then spend weeks grinding them through a committee while we argue about the return on investment. We follow managers around and teach them how to properly do a 'waste walk' and they write up a bunch of stuff they see on the floor that has zero impact on their performance. There's no such animal as a waste-free process, as Jack always beats into our heads, so there's always going to be things to write down on a list. What's the point? This is starting to get frustrating."

"Starting to, eh" said Gary with a grim smile. "You can feel it, can't you? That sinking feeling that we're starting to lose the teams. The energy we used to have. The enthusiasm. The support.

We used to have people asking us when their lines or their teams were going to be able to do a workshop with us. Now, we just get friendly waves and chit chat. It seems like everybody's keeping their heads down and just trying to get through the day without having more dumped on them. I feel for them and I completely understand their reaction. This is our fault Kelli, this is all our fault. We're supposed to be leading the charge and instead we're doing more and more of this bureaucratic nonsense." Gary's arm swept the length of the production control board.

"Hey, that's crap and you know it," said Kelli hotly, "we've got absolutely *zero* choice in this Gary. This stuff has been jammed down our throats by corporate and we're doing our best to protect the floor and keep the Veronicas of the world happy."

"I know all of that Kelli," said Gary, "but the teams sure don't. All they know is that the Continuous Improvement department keeps churning out demand after demand and they're starting to get tired of it."

"So what do we do about it?"

"I don't know kid, I don't know."

As Gary and Kelli stood in front of the production control board, Thanh and Dean came up the aisle. Thanh was carrying a large stack of eleven by seventeen inch sheets of colorful graphs and charts. They stopped at the production control board and Thanh started to take down the different audit result graphs from the board.

"Hey gang," from Dean, "looking at the bad news are we? Guess I can't blame you for looking like sourpusses." Gary and Kelli simply regarded Dean in silence. Thanh tried not to notice anyone as he traded out the old results for the new.

"But," continued Dean, "in your defense, I gotta say I like the nifty little programs youse guys wrote to automate the graphing of these audits. I had wonder-boy Thanh zap them over to our pointy-heads in IT to copy them. Nice"

"What do you mean by 'bad news,'" asked Gary.

"Your audits Gar, your audits," answered Dean. "Look here, your 5S running average looks like it's stuck in the low sixes. Shiloh's have been in the mid to high eights for the last few months. Look here, your waste walks have been way over the limit and youse are so far behind on your suggestions I doubt you'll be in the bonus range."

"Can you tell me, exactly," said Gary, "the difference between a six and an eight on this 5S audit's running average?"

"Uh, that would be *two*, Gary, I think the difference is two," said Dean sarcastically, smiling at his own cleverness.

"No," pressed Gary, "I mean the *real* difference. What is the real difference? When we launched 5S, we never kept score. We kept it simple. Binary. On or Off. It is or it isn't. If something was out of standard, get it back in standard. If it needed some problem solving, we'd do some problem solving. We only standardized what we felt was critical. Now, we just walk around with a clipboard and a scorecard and look for missing trashcans or fixtures slightly out of their designated area. We put tape around staplers and label them 'stapler' to comply with the new online 'Office Lean 5S Global Best Practice Standards,' we generate reams of data that get dumped into spreadsheets that we then post like wallpaper all over the shop. Instead of people working on real problems they spend their time figuring out a way to beat the system or score higher on an audit."

"So, what's your point?" asked Dean.

"My point," said Gary, "is that we're choking this place with non-value added work. This new regime of endless audits around useless measures is stomping all over the spark we've spent so much time and energy trying to create."

"Ooh," said Kelli, "poetic analogy. Well said."

"Thank you," replied Gary.

"Look kids," said Dean, "I don't know how to make this any simpler for youse."

"You know that's not a word, right," asked Kelli, "*youse*."

"Whatever shrimp," sneered Dean, "bottom line is this joint is way behind what we're doing at Shiloh so I wouldn't be surprised if your Christmas bonus checks don't buy *youse* guys more than a tank of gas."

"We're way behind on these made up metrics, you mean," said Gary, with a little heat in his voice.

"*Corporate* metrics pop," corrected Dean.

By now Thanh had finished replacing all of the charts with those containing current information. As Gary and Kelli had observed, most of the metrics had started to flatten, some near the target levels and some still a good distance away.

"See, lookit these," continued Dean with a head twist and a shoulder shrug, "it's like I been sayin,' not a single metric at your target. Every day I'm here I tell everybody I see that they're not makin' the grade. Nobody listens. Not the teams, not the supervisors. Nobody."

"Maybe it's your delivery," suggested Gary.

"And maybe," said Gary, "youse guys just ain't got what it takes to be world class. Whatever. I could care less. It's ain't gonna affect my bonus none."

"What's not going to affect your bonus," asked Charlie as he walked up to the group assembled in front of the production control board. Dean's demeanor immediately changed from full swagger to nervous.

"Uh, nothing Charlie, nothing. I was just talking with these guys about the performance around here on the corporate continuous improvement global best practice metrics."

"Uh huh," said Charlie as he pulled up his safety glasses and put on his reading glasses. He bent down to look at the different charts and graphs displayed on the production control board. After scanning them a moment, he turned to address the group.

"So," Charlie began, standing up to his full height and putting his massive hands on his hips, "it looks like we're still short of the target and some metrics are trending flat. What, Mr. Berzani, do you recommend we do here, what with you being our corporate Master Lean Six Sigma Sensei an all."

"Like I been tellin' everybody here," answered Dean, sweeping his hand to take in the entire shop, "all youse gotta do is follow the standard. I don't know what's wrong with some of these people, ya know? It's like they can't follow simple directions. They keeps askin' stupid questions and don't never do what I tells 'em. How do you expect to get higher scores like that?"

"Mr. Berzani," said Charlie in a low voice as he stepped in front of Dean and dropped a massive hand on his shoulder, "I'm going to do you the biggest favor of your life."

"Wha – what's that?" said Dean nervously as he bent under the weight of Charlie's massive arm.

"I'm going to forget," continued Charlie, "that you used the word 'stupid' when talking about my teams here. I don't know what you're used to getting away with over at Shiloh, but let me tell you this once, and *only* once," Kelli could see Charlie's thumb starting to push into Dean's shoulder directly on his collar bone, making him wince, "that if I hear from one of my team members that you've been rude, condescending, or just an ass in general, then you and me are going to have a problem, an intensely *personal* problem, do you understand me, Mr. Berzani? You seem to take some strange satisfaction in messing with my family here and I do *not* appreciate it."

The look on Dean's face was a mixture of pain, fear, and shock. His shoulder felt like it was caught in a vice. He looked around for any kind of help or support but was met with stony gazes from Kelli, Gary, and Thanh.

"Yeah, yeah, I get it Charlie, I get it," stammered Dean. Charlie let go of Dean's shoulder and bent down so that their faces were six inches apart.

"I will also need from you," said Charlie in a low, slow voice, his lips curling up revealing white teeth in a menacing look, "a plan to support my teams here to ensure that all of the targets are met by year's end. I want it on my desk by the end of the week. Is that clear to you Mr. Berzani?"

Gary said nothing as Dean looked furtively around for any kind of support, realizing none was forthcoming. Even Kelli had to admit, she hadn't seen Charlie like this before. He'd been wound up, sure, but not truly angry. This, she thought, was beyond angry. Dean looked to Thanh but only got a hard stare and a half smile in return.

"End of the week," said Dean, retreating, "sure thing Charlie. Easy. No problem." With that Dean whirled from the production control board and fled down the main aisle toward the front entrance and safety from these obviously insane people. He had his car keys in his hand before he hit the double doors and was vigorously massaging his shoulder.

"And good riddance," said Kelli.

"Short round," said Charlie, still in a low voice, "this is serious. He's the least of my problems. Ever since the merger the executive committee has been scratching for cost cuts anywhere they can find them. Even this," pointing at the charts on the board, "is fair game. They're talking right now about separating about half of the workforce and bringing in temps. Canteen service is going to be outsourced before the end of the year."

"My God," said Kelli, "what about Mary, what about Suzy, and the rest of them? Mary's been here almost as long as you!"

"Longer," said Charlie, "by two months. And I don't know. I truly don't. Right now all I know is they're putting together the packages. Zachary Flanders is now part of the process, so I know the packages will be fair."

"Fair," demanded Kelli, "how is that fair? These people are mindlessly slashing costs and for what? How short term can you think?"

"It's the thought of an IPO short round," said Charlie, "it's got everybody trying to cook the books and make the numbers look better to get a higher price when this place goes public. We're chasing all sorts of ratios like direct to indirect, supplies, raw materials, you name it."

"So," continued Kelli, "we're going to destroy this place so the execs and the private equity people can make a tidy profit and who cares what happens then? Is that it?"

"Not quite," said Charlie, "but yeah, we're getting pressure to make our numbers look better. I'm glad Zack is part of this, I truly am. I've gotta believe he's the only voice in that room that knows a company is a whole lot more than numbers on a piece of paper. It's a family."

"The great companies," said Thanh. "The great companies have always had a sense of family," said Thanh. "Any book you read on companies that have been successful over the long term do not *ever* do what we're doing now."

"You read too much," said Kelli, now in a dark mood.

"You should try it," said Thanh, trying to cheer his friend up, "it doesn't hurt and you actually learn things. If you get stuck on a word, I'd be happy to help you through it."

"I'll punch you in the head later, now let's go back to the office and keep getting you through the online part of your training," said Kelli, not taking the bait.

The group separated and went their own way, as Charlie headed to his office to keep trying to find more cost to squeeze from the organization, Kelli and Thanh headed back to the office leaving Gary standing in front of the production control board looking again at the metrics for the shop. How, he wondered, have we gotten to this point and how could this situation possibly get *any* worse?

Fate should never be tempted…

```
TDSTMP:     080815.0900Z
PRTY:       BROKEN ARROW

SNDR:       KOROMO BASE

TRGT:       GHQ

SITREP:     PERIMETER HAS BEEN
            BREACHED. REPEAT PERIMETER
            HAS ---


[TRANSMISSION INCOMPLETE - UNABLE TO
RE-ESTABLISH COMMUNICATION WITH
KOROMO BASE. ALL COMMUNICATIONS ARE
DOWN]
```

Chapter 10

August 8, 2015

Jack walked through the double doors from the shop floor up to the office area, heading for Steve Bucholtz', the Vice President of Manufacturing, office. Steve had an office created for himself at Amalgamated after the merger was announced and had displaced half of the accounting team to make room for what the Amalgamated people quietly called the 'Taj Mahal to ego.' Jack had never been in Steve's office nor had he seen it, given Steve's penchant for always keeping his door closed, disinviting anyone from simply dropping by. When asked about his lack of an open door policy, he reportedly quipped that people with an open door have no idea what their job is or what they're supposed to be doing.

The only way you spent time in Steve's office, Veronica excepted, was to be given an invitation, and getting an invitation was usually considered a bad thing as Steve tended to only deliver bad news and scathing reviews to the people at Amalgamated. With this in mind, Jack knocked on Steve's door, which was a custom-made mahogany monstrosity with oversized bronze hinges and a door handle that looked like it came from an ancient Spanish mission. Jack could hear voices inside the office and assumed that Veronica was inside, planning on how to further 'improve' the situation at Amalgamated prior to the IPO, which was now rumored to be happening sometime before the end of the year. He stood for a full minute before he knocked again, this time he rapped hard enough to sting his knuckles.

"Hold on," he heard a muffled from inside the office. Jack continued to stand outside the closed door for another two minutes before it finally swung inward on its massive hinges. Staring at Jack was Dean Berzani, wearing his usual half-sneer, shrugging his shoulders and twitching his head in his usual 'goombah' style.

"'bout time," said Dean as he ushered Jack into Steve's office. Jack could see that Steve was wearing one of his usual, too-tight shirts with the top two buttons open, his acid-washed jeans, and an enormous wristwatch. Jack's suspicions were confirmed when he saw Veronica sitting leisurely in an ornate leather chair next to Steve's desk. But, to call it a simple desk is to dishonor the majesty of what Jack was looking at. The main desk was easily eight feet wide by four feet deep with inlays of gold foil and hand-tooled leather, stained a deep, rich color that matched his office door, the desk having curved surfaces on every side; not a right angle to be found. There was also a companion piece, nearly as large, to Steve's left. Jack could see the drawer fronts that had exotic hardware and wondered how many thousands of hours it took skilled craftsmen to make these amazing pieces of furniture. Jack also quickly thought of his own grey cast-iron desk that was nearly the same age as he.

"Sit down Hartmann," said Steve, gesturing to a chair in front of his desk. Jack walked over to the designated chair and sat down. The chairs were more of the lounge variety, so that when Jack was seated, his head was barely above the top of Steve's desk, with Steve himself sitting almost a full foot higher than Jack. So he's now sitting in judgment, thought Jack.

"You're here," began Steve, "because frankly your Continuous Improvement department here at Amalgamated has been less than impressive and I'm going to make some changes."

"How do you mean," asked Jack, immediately wary of the situation. He looked quickly between Dean and Veronica and noticed they had the same menacing grin on their faces.

"I mean," said Steve, now squinting down at Jack, "that you have only managed to do one Kaizen Major Process Re-engineering Blast. That was back in May and it looks like you haven't even finished all of the open items identified from the workshop." Steve was looking at two pieces of paper and Jack could see they were from the Kaizen list aggregator, the piece of software that Charlie had to 'lease' from the consulting group. Another indignity piled on top of the painful process.

"We've completed all of the items that were identified except the capital investment," said Jack.

Steve stared at the papers for a long while, flipping from one to the other while Veronica and Dean simply sat quietly, waiting for permission to speak. Steve finally let out a sigh and looked down at Jack, now visibly uncomfortable in his chair and doing his best to sit as high as he could while regarding Steve's half-lidded stare.

"I don't need to hear excuses," continued Steve, "as to why you and your team can't complete the simplest of tasks. With Dean's expert certifications and leadership, you and your team should be doing at least one, maybe two Process Re-Engineering Blasts a month." Dean looked at Jack through narrowed eyes and a half-smirk played across his face.

"A month," said Jack, incredulity creeping into his voice.

"Yes, a month," said Steve, his voice slowing to emphasize the word 'month.' "Shiloh has been knocking off one or two a month for the last four years, isn't that right Dean?"

Steve was now looking at Dean, who affected a serious look, stroked his chin a few times, and looked at Steve with a hard smile. "Yep, that's about right by my reckoning," said Dean.

"And," continued Steve, "by *my* reckoning, with each Blast netting at least a quarter million, Shiloh is banking anywhere between four and six million a year on the team's efforts. You, on the other hand, Mr. Hartmann, have only managed to complete one Blast, netting a paltry two hundred thousand dollars to the bottom line."

"But Steve," began Jack.

"Mr. Bucholtz, Jack," interrupted Veronica, "you may address him as Mr. Bucholtz. Don't be rude as well as incompetent." Jack could feel his neck and ears catch fire. So that's what this is, thought Jack, an ad-hoc performance review of him, and by extension, his entire team.

"My apologies," said Jack evenly, "I don't mean to be disrespectful. But based on my inquiries, Shiloh's bottom line isn't showing those benefits. At least nowhere near the four to six million you say. I think we should be focused more on what we can do to really affect improvements."

"Your inquiries," said Steve with eyebrows raised. He slowly looked to Veronica who only shrugged her shoulders and then looked back at Jack. "Mr. Hartmann," continued Steve, his tone menacing, "I find it disconcerting that you are trying to excuse your lack of performance by making absurd claims that have no basis in reality."

"But the numbers say," said Jack.

"The numbers say," interrupted Steve, "what I damn well say they say. Period. End of story. You read me?" Steve's face was a mask of anger and condescension. Jack could only nod. No allies, no defense. Nothing he could say would change this meeting, so he quietly steeled himself for whatever was going to come next.

"Good," said Steve, "Now let's get back to business. You're not stupid Jack, so stop acting that way. We've got an IPO coming up in the next few months and we've got to get Amalgamated's performance up to the same level as Shiloh's or we're going to get a lot of valuation kicked out of the offering. That, Mr. Hartmann, is something I simply can *not* let happen."

Jack noticed that Veronica was either nodding in agreement with Steve or shaking her head when he said something negative. Dean simply leaned against the massive bookcase against the wall and regarded Jack like a hungry lion regards a lame zebra.

"We've been," continued Steve as he propped his feet up on the far end of his desk, "cutting everywhere we can find any fat, as you know. We're getting rid of services that we can no longer afford, such as the food services group, the facility maintenance group, most of the logistics group, and consolidating departments and dumping the excess costs."

"People," said Jack, unable to stop himself.

"What?" said Steve, looking at Jack.

"You said costs," said Jack, "but they're people. Some of them are the longest-serving people here at Amalgamated. People that have been here since Ezekiel Flanders was still running the company. You call them costs but they're people. They're part of the Amalgamated family. We've always had a strong sense of family here, and I say that as one of the newest hires at Amalgamated. You can see it everywhere, the way people work together, the way they talk, the way they handle whatever gets thrown at them. Good times or bad, they've always been able to count on one another, and now that's getting torn up and thrown into the dumpster." Jack's voice trailed off as his words sank deeply into his own thinking. He knew he was right, that the Amalgamated he knew was slowly dying. The culture that brought him here was being destroyed; a culture that had been built over eight decades was coming crashing down in a matter of months. How is that even possible? Jack's reflection was cut short by Steve.

"Very impressive speech, Jack, but unfortunately not very firmly rooted in reality," Steve said. "Family? Really? Come on Jack, be serious, do you think Wall Street really cares about a company's culture? If they did, there'd be a metric for it. No, Mr. Hartmann, we need to make the hard decisions to guarantee that this newly merged company is set on a footing that will last another hundred years. And sometimes hard decisions require letting people go." Steve was gesturing in the general direction of the shop floor. "We've begun the involuntary separations already. And, thanks to the 'input' from Zachary Flanders, the packages are *way* too generous, in my opinion." Veronica was pursing her lips and nodding in agreement. Jack looked to Dean who, to his surprise, had a genuine look of confusion on his face. Why?

"We're giving," said Steve, "full pensions and, depending on years of service, up to three years' salary as severance. It's going to cost us millions Jack, millions that should be used to prop up our balance sheet, not given away."

"Don't you think," asked Jack, "that people should be able to leave here with dignity after a lifetimes' service?"

"That's not my problem Jack. But, enough of that," continued Steve, "we're here to figure out how to get you and your group back on track so you can at least contribute something prior to the IPO. So here's what we're going to do. I've charged Dean with coming up with a recovery plan for this site that will get at least another million in savings. He's been here long enough to be able to put his finger on waste in just about every department. Your job, Mr. Hartmann, will be to implement his plan without deviation. Do you understand these instructions as I've described them?" Steve reclined back in his chair, and clasped his hands behind his head.

"Yes, I understand," said Jack, still feeling the heat of his ears and neck.

"Good," said Steve, now giving Jack a quick smile and a wink, "now that we've got that behind us, I'll let you get back to your team. Good day Mr. Hartmann." With that, Steve gestured to the massive mahogany door. Jack pushed himself up out of the lounge chair and headed for the exit. He pulled the massive door toward him and walked through.

"Close it," he heard Steve say behind him. Jack dutifully pulled the door shut and heard the massive latch catch in the striker. He could hear Steve's muffled voice followed by peals of laughter coming from Veronica. Jack stood there for a minute listening to the muffled laughter of Steve and Veronica. Oddly, he didn't hear Dean.

* * *

Jack walked down the main aisle of the factory, exchanging waves with team members and supervisors as they recognized each other. Jack couldn't bring himself to return the smiles; the afterglow of the meeting with Steve had dampened his spirits markedly. He was effectively told that his team wasn't performing at a level that was deemed 'acceptable' and that he had better improve his performance or his entire group might be eliminated. That thought bothered Jack immensely.

How could any rational person think that what was done here at Amalgamated wasn't a good thing? Jack and his team had focused on a pilot line; they had trained up the workforce and had full commitment from the leadership team. As the line's performance improved, Charlie had funded the new position of team leader, allowing for even more improvement to take place. The operator skill matrices had allowed the team to go from a 'this is my job' mentality to 'these are the jobs in the team.' Each team member now had an accurate assessment of their own skills and where they needed to improve.

Amalgamated had even changed the pay structure to recognize and reward the internal development that was taking place beyond the typical job description. People were getting rewarded for improving themselves and the business was reaping the benefits of a more skilled, motivated workforce. True, Jack thought to himself, we'd only managed to get the one pilot line launched, but the plans were in place to begin expanding to other areas on the plant. That, however, came to a screeching halt when the merger with Shiloh had happened and Amalgamated was designated the 'support team.'

Jack could see the results of the 'corporate best practices' all around. Walking through Business Unit 3, he could see the myriad audit result charts, with full color graphs, exponentially weighted moving averages, current audit results, and another line, usually far above, showing 'Shiloh current performance,' as a slap to the local teams, disguised as an incentive. Jack saw the supervisor's desk covered in labels and tape. The stapler had a tape outline that was labeled 'stapler,' the same could be found on his monitor, keyboard, and even the mouse, which Jack found even more ridiculous, as it was an old mouse, complete with cord. Where was it going to go?

All of this was the result of the new corporate standards that made no distinction between what was critical and thus should be standardized, and what was not, which shouldn't. Everywhere Jack looked there was some new standard that had to be maintained and, more importantly, it seemed, audited and reported. Jack exited the Business Unit and made his way to the cafeteria to get himself a cup of coffee. He would, he thought, head up to the conference room on the second floor and think about all of this.

Jack walked up to the coffee pot at the end of a long counter, poured himself a medium coffee, and stuck the lid securely on the cup. He made his way to the cash register and noticed that Mary was joined by another woman. A girl, really, by the looks of her. Jack thought she barely looked like she was out of high school. She was twirling her long, blonde hair with a finger on her left hand and noisily working on a piece of chewing gum. She was staring at the touch screen on the register as though it was an alien life form, tilting her head from one side to the other, as if this motion would somehow clarify the intentions of the strange, non-communicative flat piece of glass. Jack stood silently in front of the register, watching this ritual until Mary turned back around and noticed Jack.

"Oh hi Jack," said Mary, "this is Brittany. She's part of the new canteen company that's going to be replacing us." Tiffany looked at Jack and gave him a dazzling smile as she tilted her head to one side and kept twirling her hair.

"I thought," said Jack, "that the staff was staying here until the end of the year."

"Yeah," said Mary, "so did we. But we got called into a conference room last Friday and told by some guys in very expensive suits that we'd have two weeks to train the new people and then we'd be separated. Classy move, right?" Mary's face looked more tired than Jack had ever seen. He wondered how, despite her always positive outlook, she was dealing with this. Except for one of the maintenance men, Mary was the most senior person in the building. She was walking, talking, Amalgamated history.

"I'm sorry Mary," Jack said. "I really am."

"Me too," said Mary, as she looked at Jack, "I don't need the money, you know, I just love working here. I look forward to it every morning, seeing everybody. Talking with them. They're my family Jack, you know?" A look of sadness came over Mary's face as she quietly contemplated her future. Jack wondered what she'd do now.

"Like," said Brittany, "what *size* is that coffee?" She was pointing at Jack's cup, cracking her gum and still twirling her hair.

Jack stared at Brittany a moment. The cafeteria cups all were marked either with an 's,' for small, 'm' for medium, and 'l' for large. Jack's cup clearly had an 'm' molded into the side, facing Brittany. He looked at the 'm' and then looked at Brittany. She simply stared at Jack cracking her gum and twirling her hair.

"It's a medium," Jack finally said.

Brittany started jabbing her index finger at the touch screen, recoiling after each jab like the screen was a hot stove. After the fourth jab, Brittany was rocking her head from side to side; unsure as to why the register wasn't doing her bidding. Mary came up next to her.

"No, no, honey," Mary said, "you've charged him for a sandwich and chips. We'll need to cancel this and try again."

"Whatever," huffed Brittany, "these registers are too hard to use. I'm going to tell my uncle Bob to get rid of these dumb machines and get something that, like, works."

"It's ok Brittany," said Mary, "just hit the red 'cancel' button and we'll try again. It's right there on the top right." Mary had her finger about an inch away from the screen, showing Brittany the proper place to touch.

"Whatever," said Brittany, "this is so stupid." She was still twirling her hair and jabbing at the cancel button. After four more jabs, Mary had to intervene.

"Brittany," she said patiently, "now you just rang up a bowl of soup. You see the picture there honey? It looks like a bowl of soup. You just pushed that instead of the picture of the coffee." Mary looked apologetically at Jack as he fished a dollar from his pocket and laid it down on the counter. He mouthed the words 'thank you' to Mary as he made his way to the exit, taking a sip of his coffee. As he looked back over his shoulder, he could see Mary still trying to get Brittany to ring in a medium coffee on the register.

Jack wondered if 'uncle Bob' was the owner of the new cafeteria services company that was replacing Mary, Suzy, and the rest of the Amalgamated employees in the kitchen. If so, the breaks and lunches are going to have to be extended because people aren't going to be able to get past the register in time. Amazing, Jack thought. And this was supposed to save money somehow. Bring in low-wage low-skill people and put them into an area that needs a certain level of skill and training. Brilliant.

Jack continued to sip his coffee as he walked back to his office and sat down. He wanted to check his e-mail before he headed upstairs to the conference room to think. He heard the outer office door bang open, letting in the sounds of the floor. He'd need to talk to whoever just blew in here that there's no real need to slam doors. He was just getting up from his desk when Kelli flew into view; literally. She slid to a stop in his doorway and caught herself on the frame. She was breathing hard and had a look of panic on her face that Jack hadn't seen before.

"Kelli, what –", began Jack.

"It's Gary," said Kelli breathlessly.

"What about Gary?" asked Jack, now concerned.

"They just," she gasped, "security just walked Gary out of the building."

```
TDSTMP:    080815.1045Z
PRTY:      IMMEDIATE

SNDR:      BIG EYE - AERIAL RCN

TRGT:      GHQ

SITREP:    KOROMO BASE HEAVILY DAMAGED
           AND COVERED IN SMOKE. FIRES
           APPEAR OUT OF CONTROL.
           UNABLE TO SEE SIGNS OF
           LIFE. SITUATION UNCLEAR.
           ASSUME BASE DESTROYED.
           SUGGEST RECON IN FORCE TO
           SEARCH FOR ANY SURVIVORS.

[END TRANSMISSION]
```

Chapter 11

August 8, 2015

The doors to the continuous improvement office blew open and slammed against their stops as Jack nearly ran through them. He yanked his safety glasses down on his head and began a double-time march down the main aisle up toward the front offices. Behind him in the office, Kelli began telling Thanh what she had seen. Security and Human Resources hadn't allowed anyone near Gary as he was escorted out to the parking lot, so Kelli knew nothing more than what she had seen. My God, she thought, is this really happening? Was this push to cook the financial books prior to the IPO so great that people were just being shoved out the gate to make the numbers look better? Is this what we've come to?

Jack was about halfway down the aisle when Geoff Mueller stepped out next to Business Unit 3.

"Hey Jack, I need to talk to you about…" began Geoff.

"Not now," said Jack through clenched teeth, without looking, as he kept up his blistering pace down the aisle as his mind raced. Geoff stopped and said something in reply that Jack couldn't hear as he faded in the distance behind him. Jack stopped in front of the double doors that led to the front office area and his destination; Veronica Appleton's office. He took a deep breath, then another, trying to slow his breathing and his heartrate after his walk up here, but he knew his brief explosion of energy had nothing to do with his current condition. He was angry, and he knew it. He welcomed it, let it wash over him. His thoughts turned very dark as the last five months of memories flooded his thoughts. The insults. The humiliation. The threats. Enough was enough. He took a last deep breath and yanked the door open and began walking toward Veronica's office. He got to the door and banged his knuckles loudly on the door, causing Veronica to jump as she spun in her chair to look at him. Jack could see Dean was in her office, stacking the last of six boxes against the wall. Jack guessed, correctly, that those boxes contained the contents of Gary's desk. Jack could feel his neck and ears were glowing red as he stood at the edge of Veronica's desk, planted his fists down hard, and stared at Veronica with a look of simmering rage.

"What have you done," he said slowly, staring hard at Veronica, who unconsciously pushed her chair back a few inches from her desk as she looked up at Jack.

"I don't think it's your place-" began Veronica.

"Why did you," Jack was almost screaming, "walk Gary Peterson to the door like he was nothing?!"

"Hey chill out Jackie-boy," said Dean, "gramps had worn out his welcome, right V? Plus, we didn't want him stealin' no secrets, so he gets himself the perp walk."

Jack whirled to his left, took two steps toward Dean and grabbed him by the front of the jacket and began forcing him backward toward the wall, the rage inside him now in full bloom and white hot.

"Say that again," said Jack, his nose an inch from Dean's as Dean slammed into the wall of Veronica's office hard enough to knock over a picture on a shelf. "Insult my friend again Dean. He didn't need to steal any secrets; the man was a walking *encyclopedia* of this place!" Jack curled his fists inside Dean's jacket and began to push against Dean's throat, denying him air. A look of panic came over Dean's face as he realized he couldn't release himself from Jack's grip. His eyes darted between Jack's and Veronica, who simply sat at her desk, mouth agape. Seconds seemed to last hours.

"Jack," said Kelli from behind Jack, now standing in Veronica's door, "we need to go. Now. We're late for the update meeting out on the floor." Kelli walked up to Jack and stood next to him as he simply held onto Dean's jacket. Kelli reached out and slid her fingers under his left arm, digging her nails into the soft flesh under his bicep. She squeezed hard enough that Jack winced, sucked in breath through clenched teeth, and slowly let go of Dean, whose face was bright pink from the ordeal. Jack looked at Kelli, finally, and then looked down at his arm, then his eyes met Kelli's. Kelli let go as he turned and walked out of Veronica's office: she quickly followed. Veronica had overcome her shock at the sudden savagery that had just taken place in her office, her sudden loss of power, her control. She looked at Dean standing at the wall massaging his neck, enjoying his ability to breathe again, she felt she needed to reassert some sort of authority. Control. Anything.

"Mr. Hartmann!" she called out of her office in as stern a voice as she could muster. By then Jack and Kelli had nearly reached the doors out to the production floor, "your lack of professionalism has been noted and will become part of your permanent record." Jack ignored her and kept walking. He slowed enough for Kelli to catch up, and opened the door for her as they both pulled down their safety glasses and walked through out to the floor. Jack started massaging his left arm absentmindedly. Kelli looked at him as they walked.

"Sorry about that boss," began Kelli, "but I needed to get you out of there. Nothing good was going to come of that and you know it."

"I know Kelli," said Jack, "and thank you. That was stupid on my part. I just couldn't let them walk Gary out like a common criminal. How did you know where I was?"

"Geoff Mueller came down to the office at a run and said you blew past him looking mad enough to spit nails. I figured you were looking for Veronica, and I guessed right. I still can't believe they walked Gary out."

Jack was still massaging his left arm as they turned off the main aisle and walked into the team review area of Business Unit 1. It was nice, he thought, to have people looking out for you, even if you're doing something stupid. Yes, he had a great team. No, he corrected himself, more than a team; it was truly a family. Kelli had told him that before he came here. And they had just lost a very valuable member. He was still massaging his arm as they walked.

"Is the arm ok boss-man?" asked Kelli.

"No, it's not," said Jack, frowning and raising an eyebrow as he looked at Kelli. "You've got an iron grip, has anyone ever told you that?"

"Came in handy, didn't it?"

"I guess so. I think we need to go find Gary after we get out of this review," continued Jack, "you in?"

"Absolutely. And I know just where to go, too."

Jack and Kelli approached the review area where the team was gathered and they were going through their recent performance as well as the open items list. Thanh was there and caught Kelli's eye as she walked up with Jack. Thanh raised his eyebrows questioningly and got a quick nod and a smile from Kelli. Everything's ok; for now.

The team review went on for fifty minutes until all of the items had been covered. Jack and his team had volunteered to help where they could, with Thanh offering to automate as much of the new paperwork as possible and Kelli would provide the training on how to use Thanh's home-grown programs so that the team could cut down the time it took to update all of the new audit results and charts and graphs. The meeting broke up and Jack, Kelli, and Thanh walked back toward the main aisle. Jack turned right instead of left, which was the direction of the production offices, and Kelli and Thanh followed.

"Where we goin' now boss?" asked Kelli. "Shouldn't we be heading for the exits?"

"Not yet. I want to see Charlie," said Jack, "to see if he knows what's going on."

"I am very sorry," said Thanh, "that Gary is no longer part of our team. He was a very smart man and I relied on him a lot."

"Thank you Thanh," answered Jack, "we all relied on him."

The trio arrived at the production office area and made their way through the rows of desks until they got to Taylor Smith's desk, just outside of Charlie's office. She looked up from her computer and smiled at the three of them.

"He's out Jack," began Taylor, "if you're looking for Charlie."

"He's out," parroted Jack, disappointed.

"Yeah," continued Taylor, "he left about an hour ago. He said he had some personal business to take care of and that he'd be back later. Do you want me to tell him you stopped by?"

"Sure," said Jack, "please. I'll swing by later this afternoon and see if I can find him."

"Why don't I just call your cell when he gets back," offered Taylor.

"Great, thank you Taylor," said Jack. With that, the group exchanged goodbyes and Jack and his team headed back out onto the floor.

"Thanh," said Jack, "Kelli and I are going to see if we can catch up with Gary, so I'm going to need you to mind the store here for a while. We don't have any other reviews today, so we should be fine.

"No problem Jack," said Thanh, "I can get started on the work we need to do to support Business Unit 1. I'll see you when you get back."

With that, Jack and Kelli headed for the side exit which led to the parking lot and Thanh continued back down the main aisle to their offices. Kelli already had her car keys in her hand.

* * *

Dooley's Bar and Grill was your typical watering hole in a small town. The 'grill' was added decades earlier and was shoehorned into the back corner of the bar, with the exhaust hood ducting exiting the building through a ragged cut in the cinderblock wall. Duct tape did its best to seal the opening. The outside parking space below the vent was never occupied, even though it was fairly close to the front door. Sometimes an unwary traveler would marvel at their good luck and park in that spot, only to find that the exhaust vent had dripped some form of grease-based biology experiment that usually took a strong car wash, or three, to remove. The lighting inside the bar was dim and the place had a faint odor of stale beer mixed with grease. A ceiling fan that badly needed balancing slowly creaked overhead. The three booths along the wall had red vinyl seat coverings liberally covered in duct tape where the vinyl had torn. The owners were big fans of the gray miracle-adhesive. The barstools were newer, having been replaced a few years ago, with a high back and full swivel seats. At this time of the day, the entire place was empty except for one person. Gary Peterson sat near the far end of the bar, slowly stirring the ice in his glass as he watched on TV what passed for the latest developments in the sports world.

The door opened, ringing an ancient small brass bell, and the bar was flooded with bright light. Gary looked to the source of the intrusion and saw a massive figure silhouetted against the doorframe, almost ducking as he walked in. Gary recognized Charlie Cooks at a distance and watched as he walked down the bar and pulled out the stool next to Gary's. The barstool creaked as it accepted Charlie's bulk. Charlie looked at Gary for a long moment, looked down at the drink in front of Gary, and then looked back at Gary with a raised eyebrow.

"Club soda," said Gary, "with a splash of cranberry juice. Don't worry Charlie, I'm still on the wagon."

"Glad to hear it," answered Charlie, "but after the day you just had, I doubt anybody'd blame you."

"Trish would, Charlie, and I can't have that, regardless of how my day went. Which, by the way, was amazingly dreadful. Did you know what was going on? That this was going to happen?"

"Gary," said Charlie, "I hope you know me better than that. There is absolutely *zero* chance that I would ever let anybody get treated like that."

"I know, Charlie, and I'm sorry for saying it," said Gary as he twirled his straw in his glass, "but that place has gotten pretty cutthroat since the merger and impending IPO. It's like everybody's on edge. You're either cutting something or worried you're going to be cut. Look at me."

"What, exactly," asked Charlie, "did they say when they showed up at your office?"

"Well," said Gary, "Veronica Appleton walked in followed by Tim and Andy from security, and Dean. Tim and Andy each had three boxes with them. I knew what was coming. Veronica told me that my employment was being terminated, or involuntarily separated; whatever. And she slowly explained that because I was privy to all sorts of inside information about the company, the standard two week period was being waived and I was to be walked to the door. On the way out Andy took my badge, cell phone, and office keys. I felt bad for him, you know, he had a look on his face like he was walking me to the gallows."

"Your cell phone?" asked Charlie. "Isn't that your personal cell phone?"

"Yeah," answered Gary, "but Veronica said it had work numbers and emails on it so it had to be scrubbed by the I.T. boys before it could be 'safely' returned to me. Whatever. I didn't use that thing anyway."

"Damn," was all Charlie could say, shaking his head. "We'll get it back Gary, I promise you I *will* make that happen. As soon as I get back to the shop."

"Thanks Charlie," said Gary, "I'd also like to get my pictures back too."

"Done."

"Who would've thought, Charlie, after all the years I put in at Amalgamated that I'd get walked to the door like I just robbed payroll. People must've thought the worst," said Gary smiling ruefully.

"Yeah," said Charlie, smiling, "they don't have much respect for us older folk, do they?"

"Not at all, my friend. We're just cost to them. Cost that walks in on two legs every day."

Just then Patrick Dooley, grandson of the bar's founder, walked out of the stockroom carrying a case of a local craft beer.

"Oh, hey Charlie," he said in greeting, "I didn't hear ya come in. You want your usual?"

"Why not," said Charlie looking at his watch, "I don't need to be back for another hour or so."

Patrick pulled a double old fashioned glass from behind the bar and filled it halfway with Charlie's favorite bourbon. Patrick then dropped a single ice cube into the dark amber liquid and slid it across to Charlie.

"Thanks Pat," said Charlie.

"You guys want any food?" asked Patrick, "I can fire up the grill."

"No thanks Pat, we're good," said Charlie, "we don't need the fire department showing up again when the exhaust pipe catches fire."

"Ha ha, funny man," said Patrick, "then I'm gonna go keep restocking the bar from the back. Holler if you need anything. And Gary, keep Mr. funny-bones here out of my good bourbon, will ya?"

"Sure thing Pat," said Gary, smiling.

With that, Pat walked down the bar, past the grill, and turned and went back into the stockroom to get ready for the afternoon and evening rush.

Charlie swirled his glass, watching the ice cube slowly begin to melt into the bourbon, chilling it just a bit below room temperature. Charlie had cultivated this particular taste early in his career when he had the opportunity to have lunch with Ezekiel Flanders, the company founder. Old man Flanders told everyone present that a true gentleman drank his bourbon straight, but with a cube to put just a little chill in it and bring out the flavor. Charlie wasn't sure about the flavor bit, but the ritual stuck.

"You had what, Gary" asked Charlie after a while, "over forty years?"

"Forty two," said Gary, "I came on board in March, after I finished my rehab after my car accident."

"That's right," said Charlie, "you got hired about two months before I did."

Charlie stared at his glass for a long moment before turning to regard Gary.

"You know Gary," said Charlie, "I never took the opportunity to say thank you."

"For what?" asked Gary, eyebrows arched.

"I know it was you," said Charlie simply. "Back then."

"What are you talking about Charlie?" said Gary, a perplexed look on his face.

"That day in the railyard," continued Charlie, "when those two drunk fools were trying to crack my skull. I know it was you that yelled to me. If you hadn't done that, I might've ended up with a broken back, or worse."

Gary just stared at Charlie, his mind racing back to that cool autumn day. He'd been loading up one of the massive sawmills when the word got out that the giant kid Charlie was going to be 'taught some manners.' Gary, along with the rest of the sawmill gang and receiving crew, made their way out to the railyard to watch the show. By the time Gary made his way outside, the fight had already started. Gary could see somebody was already down; it looked like Mark Williams, He saw Charlie slammed around the mid-section by Tom Jorgensen. Gary simply watched as Charlie's massive fists reached high in the sky and came down solidly on Tom's back. He saw Tom collapse like a rag doll at Charlie's feet. This was getting out of hand, Gary thought, as he saw Mark swinging a pipe wildly at Charlie. Where was security? Gary saw Charlie's left cross smash into Mark and abruptly end the fight. Serves those two idiots right, he thought. Gary was turning to go back into the building when he saw Tom moving silently behind Charlie, bringing a piece of pipe out of his coveralls and starting to swing at Charlie's exposed back. Jesus, Gary thought, he's gonna kill him. "Behind you!" he yelled, at the top of his lungs. Gary saw Charlie look into the crowd for the source of the voice and then start turning. He saw Tom's pipe crash into Charlie's back and the big kid drop to a knee. Unbelievably, Gary watched as Charlie spun and wrenched the pipe to one side and just about took Tom's head off with a wicked right. Then it was over. Gary stood silently as Charlie walked past the crowd, asking if anybody else 'needed some damn gloves.' Gary smiled, and walked back inside to get back to his job.

The fun was over. Gary made himself a mental note to never, under any circumstances, ever, get young Mr. Cooks mad at him. Ever.

"Well," said Gary, smiling, "if those two idiots wanted a fight, it was going to be a *fair* fight."

"Fair?" said Charlie, "you know those two fools had lead pipes, right?"

"True," said Gary, "but you *are* close to seven feet tall Charlie. And about the size of a Mack truck."

"I suppose," agreed Charlie, "but those were different times. I wonder whatever happened to those two clowns."

"Tom, it probably won't surprise you," said Gary, "got himself killed in a bar fight not too long after your little 'dance' in the railyard. Old Man Flanders got wind of the fight and fired both of them on the spot. A few days after he got canned, Tom was getting drunk and obnoxious one night at the honky-tonk, you know, the one that closed about ten years ago? Any way, he was mouthing off and started a fight. Of course he brought along his favorite lead pipe. Problem was, the other guy brought his gun to a lead pipe fight. Didn't end well for Tom. As far as Mark, I have no idea. He split right after he got shown the door. Didn't leave a forwarding address."

"Karma's a bitch," said Charlie, "but you know Gary, that isn't all I know about you, you know."

"What are you talking about Charlie," said Gary, now squinting at Charlie, his scarred temple and eyebrow giving him a somewhat menacing look.

"I know you weren't in any car wreck Gary, that's what I know. That famous, handsome, *squint* of yours and all," said Charlie, swirling his drink, staring at the amber liquid as it continued to melt his ice cube.

Gary unconsciously started to rub the left side of his face, next to his eyebrow, where the spider web of scars met. He regarded Charlie for a long moment, his mind racing.

"What exactly," said Gary evenly, "do you *think* you know?"

"Warrant Officer Gary Peterson," said Charlie, now looking down at Gary, "severely wounded in action in support of combat units in Operation Fishhook, during the 1970 invasion of Cambodia."

Gary sat for a moment, still rubbing his left temple. This news stunned him. He had told no-one, except his wife Trish, of his life before he joined Amalgamated. Why would Trish tell anyone?

"Jesus, who told you?" asked Gary quietly.

"You did, Gary," answered Charlie, looking down into Gary's confused face, "you did."

"There's no way I...," began Gary.

"It was one of those afternoons," interrupted Charlie, "when you were deep into a bottle of that cheap hooch you used to drink. It must've been around three or so and I get a call from Pat here, all upset, telling me to get down here and get you home before somebody called the police. You were making quite a ruckus apparently. By the time I got here, you were pretty sloshed. You were crying like a fool about something or other. To be honest, I couldn't understand much of it. As I was walking you out, you started babbling about something being 'hot.' 'The LZ is too hot' you were saying, over and over. Then you started yelling for Mike, whoever that was."

"I said that huh?" Gary was staring at the dented and scratched bar in front of him, a somber look on his face. "I don't remember any of that, which is no big surprise. And then what?" pressed Gary.

"And, you know my wife runs the county library system, right," asked Charlie.

"Yes, of course I do, what does.." said Gary, suddenly connecting the dots. "Oh, crap…."

"She's amazing at research. She loves it. It's like catnip to the woman. The fewer the clues the better, in her opinion. Simply amazing. She would blow your mind, trust me. I gave her what I got from you, and after a while and some serious digging, she figured out that you were a chopper pilot in Viet Nam. You musta been a damn kid back then. She tracked down your service records and found the citations and awards."

"Great," said Gary flatly, looking into his drink.

"She found out," continued Charlie, "Warrant Officer Peterson, that you were flying those old Huey helicopters in support of the Cambodia invasion when your ship got blasted. From the reports it said you had just unloaded ammunition and supplies and were loading up wounded soldiers when all hell broke loose at the landing zone. The North Vietnamese managed to get close enough to shoot the hell out of all the helicopters on the ground. Only a couple of birds made it out. Your co-pilot, Mike Rockwell, got killed instantly and your bird got shot all to pieces. You managed to get out of there and head back to your base, trailing smoke the whole way. You crashed onto the base, destroying the chopper and two buildings along the way, but everyone made it except Rockwell."

"Yeah," said Gary in a whisper, staring for a while in the distance at something a long, long time ago. "Mike never had a chance. Never knew what hit him, thank God. Grenades and heavy machine-gun fire raked the LZ as we were pulling the last of the wounded aboard. He took the brunt of the explosion, and slowed down the shrapnel enough so that it just sledge-hammered my head, instead of killing me, too. I don't remember much from the flight back, I was going in and out of consciousness. Good reflexes and great training, I suppose. I just remember the ground coming up really fast and hauling back with everything I had left. There was a crunch. A lot of yelling. I remember somebody yanking open the door on my side of the cockpit. More yelling. Then nothing. Somehow we made it. Next thing I remember, I was in a field hospital wrapped in bandages down to my chest."

"You got yourself," said Charlie, "a Silver Star for gallantry and a Purple Heart. Rockwell got his posthumously."

"And don't forget this little memento," said Gary, pointing to the left side of his face.

"Jesus Gary," said Charlie in a low, slow voice, "that makes you some sort of war hero, doesn't it? Why'd you keep that a secret?"

"Because," said Gary, "I wasn't a war hero. We all went over there for different reasons. But when we got there, we were fighting for each other. The guy next to you, you know? I just wanted to live. To survive. To make it back. I was just doing my job. We all were. We were fighting for each other over there."

"You say so," said Charlie, taking another sip of bourbon.

"Those days when you guys used to come and get me," said Gary, "those weren't good times for me. After Trish died. I'm not proud of how I handled her death."

"I know," said Charlie, "and to be truthful Gary, I didn't have a lot of respect for you then, neither. Miss Patricia scolded me and told me I needed to put myself into your shoes, and walk for a while, before I started judging you. So I did. That woman's amazingly smart, you know? I gotta admit, I can't imagine what I'd do without her. I didn't know how you kept going. So, I just kept coming to get you whenever Pat called."

"Thank you, Charlie, for that. I don't think I ever really said thank you. My biggest problem, back then, was that I got stuck," said Gary.

"Stuck?" asked Charlie.

"When Trish died, I didn't know what to do. I'd wake up every morning expecting to see her lying next to me. When I didn't see her, I just didn't see any reason to give a damn about anything. We had plans. We were going to travel around Europe and see ancient castles and go sailing on the Mediterranean. We had so much life ahead of us and so many plans. When I buried her, I couldn't see how I could ever move forward. So I got stuck. And I crawled into a bottle to try and dull the pain. And it was comfortable, enough, I guess, so I just stayed there. Stuck in that bottle."

"Until," said Charlie, "your run-in out in the boonies with the quote *deer* unquote," said Charlie as he held up both hands and pantomimed the quotation marks.

"Yeah," laughed Gary, "that damned deer. Anyway, after surviving that little encounter with nature, I got sober and stayed that way."

"So now what," asked Charlie, "you still stuck?"

"No," said Gary, "I'm not stuck anymore. To tell you the truth Charlie, I was probably going to turn in my retirement at the end of the year anyway. I still want to do those things that Trish and I talked about. It won't be the same, but I think Trish would approve, you know?"

"Sounds good to me," said Charlie.

"And," Gary went on, "with this 'immediate involuntary separation' garbage that went down today, I now have three full years of salary, plus my full pension, to fund my travels."

"So," said Charlie, "a good end to a rotten day?"

"Something like that, I guess."

"Well," said Charlie, lifting his massive frame out of the barstool, "I'd better get going."

"Back to the shop?" asked Gary.

"No," said Charlie, "I need to go see an old friend. We haven't talked in a little while and we need to have a serious conversation about the future."

Charlie pulled a ten dollar bill from his pocket and dropped it on the bar.

"Knowing Jack and short round," said Charlie, "I bet they're on their way here, especially since they took your cell phone when they walked you to the door. And if short round is drivin' they should be here any minute. That girl's driving scares me silly."

"Me too, and you're probably right," said Gary, "especially since I didn't even get to say goodbye to anybody."

"And," said Charlie, "I don't' want to be here when they blow in, so I'm headin' out the back way. I'll probably take the back roads too, 'cause they might recognize my truck. No sense them knowing we had a little talk. Short round will claw it out of me, and I don't want to have to deal with that. So, I'll take your favorite back roads, the one with all the deer. And do me a favor Gary, when you get done with all of your travels, or quest, or whatever you're going to go and do, stop by and see Miss Patricia and me. We haven't been exactly close all these years, but that doesn't mean it's too late to try. She'd love to hear about Italy. And be sure to invite me to your going away party, whenever that is. We'll be there."

"I will Charlie, and thank you. And drive safe, okay, those stupid deer out there are natural born killers," said Gary with a grin, "they just *look* cute and fuzzy."

"Natural born killers," said Charlie, eyebrows raised, "why Gary Peterson, those 'stupid deer' may have just saved your life all those years ago, don't you think?"

With that Charlie walked out the back door, leaving Gary alone with his thoughts. Saved his life, eh? Well, maybe they did, Charlie, maybe they did. He shook his head and smiled as he took another sip of his club soda. Only the ancient, creaking ceiling fan kept him company for the next few minutes. He noticed his ice was almost gone and wondered when Pat was going to come back from his inventorying duties.

He looked back toward the front door and saw a black blur flash by the slits afforded by the full length shade pulled in front of the glass to keep the lighting low. He heard gravel crunch under tires. Kelli was here, probably with a terrified Jack riding shotgun hanging on for dear life. Gary grinned at the thought of Jack's face as Kelli did her best Ferrari driver impersonation. He heard the muffled sound of car doors closing and kept his gaze averted so he wouldn't be blinded when they came through. The door flew open, ringing the ancient brass bell and Gary looked back to the door in time to see Kelli running at him, with Jack standing in the doorway. He stood up in time to catch Kelli's full speed hug without both of them toppling to the floor. She seemed to be trying to crush the air from his lungs as she let out a muffled sob into his chest. "It's ok kid, it's ok, everything is going to be ok," he said as he hugged his friend. "Come on now. We're ok."

```
TDSTMP:     083115.0815Z
PRTY:       IMMEDIATE

SNDR:       KOROMO BASE

TRGT:       GHQ

SITREP:     CENTER HELD. ENEMY IN FULL
            RETREAT. REINFORCEMENTS
            ARRIVED IN TIME TO REPEL
            FINAL ASSAULT. REQUEST
            URGENT RESUPPLY. PATROLS
            OUT TO ABANDONED FIREBASES
            TO ASSESS AND SEARCH FOR
            SURVIVORS.

[END TRANSMISSION]
```

Chapter 12

August 31, 2015

Jack was sitting at his desk looking at the latest results from the audits conducted out on the floor in the various business units. Before him was spread a kaleidoscopic display of color, with various greens, blues, reds, yellows and oranges. Last week a new 'global best practice' had been rolled from Shiloh to Amalgamated, with all the new key performance indicators and audit charts now displaying *five* distinct color bands. You were in the 'red' zone if you weren't hitting the target. Next is the 'orange' band, where you still weren't hitting the target but you had a plan that had less than a 50% chance of being met. Next came the 'yellow' band, which meant you weren't hitting the target but had a plan in place that was deemed to have a better than 50% chance of being successful. The 'green' zone came next, which said you were achieving the target. The top, and final band, was the 'blue' zone where you were achieving the targets by more than 20% and were projecting to finish the fiscal year there. What an amazing waste of ink, Jack thought, shaking his head. Why would we go to such lengths simply to show that a broom hadn't been on its newly 'standardized' hook the last three times it was checked? Why wouldn't we just talk to the team and find out where they'd prefer to keep the broom? How much was this latest trip down bureaucratic lane going to diminish the capability of his team to help the floor truly improve? Thankfully Thanh and Kelli had been able to heavily automate these new charts and graphs, but the floor was still grumbling about the new 'best practices.'

"Hey boss-man," said Kelli from his open door, "whatcha lookin' at?"

Jack looked up at Kelli and returned her smile and then looked back down at the menagerie of charts and graphs spread across his desk.

"You know Kelli," replied Jack, "I don't honestly know. I'm trying to figure out this new reporting methodology and it's giving me a bit of a headache."

"I hear you," said Kelli, "but thankfully Thanh and I were genius enough to figure out how to dump the audit data and put it into these nifty new full-color glossy charts." Kelli tilted her head, batted her eyelashes and smiled at Jack, waiting for his response. Jack continued to look down at his desk, still trying to digest yet another 'new normal.' Kelli continued to hold her pose, waiting for Jack to look up. When he didn't, she cleared her throat to get his attention. Twice.

"Hmm?" said Jack, looking over at Kelli and seeing her 'I'm waiting' face. "Oh, sorry Kelli, yes, you and Thanh really did an amazing job automating this stuff. My concern is that we're going to be alienating the teams even more with all of these new metrics and graphs. Their original line boards were fairly simple, these new charts and graphs are," Jack's voice trailed off as he waved his arm over his desk and the sea of color.

"The waste of over-processing?" asked Kelli, helpfully.

Jack sighed and looked back down at his desk, still trying to wrap his head around what lay in front of him. "I suppose so," said Jack, "but we're backed into a corner on this one. I argued that we should trial this new material, run a pilot in one of the business units and get some feedback, but I got shot down. We just grab the really big lever and pull and hope for the best."

"And waste a lot of ink," added Kelli.

Jack looked at Kelli and silently nodded. This was yet another nail in the coffin of the Amalgamated efforts on their journey. Culture change was coming, all right, but it certainly wasn't a culture that Jack was hoping to build. It was a culture built on audits, mindless following of rules, and a fair amount of fear wrapped in the feel-good platitudes of 'accountability.'

"Speaking of wasting money," said Kelli, interrupting Jack's dismal line of thought, "do you have the five bucks you owe me from Gary's party?"

Gary's retirement party had been last week. It took almost three weeks to set up, given that all of the senior managers in the facility had wanted to attend. Kelli and Thanh moved heaven and earth to get enough white space cleared into calendars that all who wanted to could attend. Some came and left early and others came and left late. Very late. The party had started at Dooley's, with most of the chairs and tables cleared out so everyone could mix and mingle with Gary easily. Once Dooley's had reached closing time, the tour bus that Charlie had rented for the occasion took the revelers over to the local Coney Island restaurant that stays open round the clock. Kelli had demanded to drive, but thankfully Charlie wrestled her back to a seat of her own.

Everybody had a good time and a raucous dart game sprung up at the back of the restaurant, with Kelli dominating the competition. Her only loss was to Pat Cooks, and that was probably because Miss Patricia limited herself to chardonnay at Dooley's while Kelli was engaged in boilermaker races with a few of the braver men present. Jack had assumed that after a few of those, Kelli's aim would be off and he challenged her to a game of darts. He quickly went up by thirty two points and then brazenly suggested that they make a 'gentleman's wager.' Kelli simply smiled, said 'sure,' and proceeded to throw bullseye after bullseye, winning by over a hundred points. After the game she gave Jack her best eyelash-batting and impish grin and stuck out her hand. Much to Jack's chagrin, his wallet was empty from the night's reveling. He promised to give Kelli her money next week in lieu of his grandfather's watch, which she had been eyeing as an alternate prize. After some cajoling, she accepted.

"Yes, Kelli, yes," said Jack as he reached into his pocket, "I have your money right here." He took out a five dollar bill and extended it to Kelli. "Does your head still hurt?"

"Yep," she said simply as she pocketed the bill, "For the next day and a half all I ate was Ibuprofen. I think I'm getting too old for that kind of stuff. Ugh."

"By 'stuff' you mean dropping a shot of house whiskey into a twenty two ounce frosted beer mug and slamming the concoction down in a race with whomever challenged you to the fevered chants of the assembled crowd?" asked Jack.

"Didn't lose did I?" asked Kelli. "I didn't have to buy all night, except the shot I sent Gary, and I made like forty bucks throwing darts."

"Congratulations," said Jack with a wry grin.

"But yes," continued Kelli, "I was a hurting puppy the whole weekend. But at least we sent Gary off properly. Thanh and I even helped him set up an Instagram account so we can keep track of him on his travels."

There had been a collection, led by Thanh and Kelli, to get Gary the latest smart phone and retire his current phone, which was circa 1995. At Dooley's, there was a brief ceremony where Gary handed over his flip phone to Kelli, who placed it into an overnight mailing bag marked 'Nokia Museum of Ancient Technology' and he was presented with its shiny new replacement. Before too many rounds had been bought, Thanh and Kelli showed Gary how to use the different apps and showed him how to keep everybody up to speed on his travels.

"That was impressive, I must admit," said Jack. "Everybody gave Gary such a hard time because he had that antiquated flip phone, but he seemed to take to the new smart phone like a duck to water."

"Yeah, it was hilarious when he showed Zack Flanders his shiny new phone and Zack pulled the exact same phone out of his own pocket. What is Flanders, like ninety years old?"

"Eighty four," said Jack, "and yes, I admit I was surprised to see Zack was up on all of the new technology. He said it was a great way to keep up with his grand kids."

"I guess so," said Kelli, "it was really nice of him to come to say goodbye to Gary. He seemed a little sad that Gary's career ended the way it did. I mean, what should he expect? He knew what was going to happen with the merger, didn't he?"

"I don't think," said Jack, "that he expected that the merged company would go on a mission to slash costs and force an IPO. I have to believe that if all of this were laid out beforehand, we probably wouldn't have merged. Zack and his father, Ezekiel, have spent their entire lives building a culture of trust and respect and I seriously doubt they'd let it be torn apart chasing a short-term profit."

"Yeah," said Kelli, "thank the private equity people for that. They want to make, what, thirty or forty percent on their 'investment' before they dump their stake after the IPO?"

"Fifty," said Jack. "Their bogey is a fifty percent net profit after they sell their ten percent after the IPO."

"Heartless slime," said Kelli.

"Now Kelli," said Jack, "this is all above board. You can't be surprised by this. Any time a merger happens, you don't just happily go along with the new company. You've got, essentially, two radically different cultures thrown into the same room with conflicting goals. It's just that our culture is being torn down by the combined weight of the private equity guys and the Shiloh leadership team."

"So eight decades of culture," said Kelli, "can be torn down in a matter of months. Is that it?"

"I wouldn't have thought so Kelli, but yes, it certainly looks like it can be," said Jack.

"That stinks," said Kelli. "This place was amazing. It wasn't perfect, sure, but you got the sense that when we had to really come together to pull something off, we could do it. Now, you're worried that if one of your new 'best practice' indicators drops into the yellow, or perish forbid, orange, you're going to get ranked by HR as a 'C Level' player and canned."

"I know," said Jack, thinking about the new A-B-C ranking methodology that was being rolled across Amalgamated by Veronica Appleton and her 'henchmen,' as Kelli referred to them so often, despite Jack's admonishments against using terms like that.

"Ah well, I'm going to go get a coffee before this gets too depressing," said Kelli as she turned to leave.

"Coffee?" asked Jack. "I thought you always got one of those caramel mocky sweet somethings."

"It's a triple, venti, half-sweet, non-fat, caramel macchiato. And no, I don't get those anymore. Our new cafeteria geniuses can barely get the coffee right, let alone anything complicated. I just dump a lot of cream and sugar in it." Kelli began to twirl her hair with a finger and make cracking sounds like she was chewing gum loudly with her mouth open. She cocked her head to the left and then to the right, mimicking Brittany, the new cafeteria register girl. "Tiffany tends to get a bit overwhelmed, if you know what I mean."

"Brittany, Kelli, it's Brittany," corrected Jack.

"Whatever," retorted Kelli, "at least they're screwing things up so badly that the transition has been postponed until the end of September. Mary's trying, but those girls aren't the sharpest tools in the shed. But, gotta cut cost before the big IPO, right?"

"I'm not sure Kelli, but I'm guessing that's why Charlie has been out of the office so much lately. He's working with the bean counters and private equity guys to get this whole thing finalized."

"Yeah," said Kelli, "and did you notice how much time Zack Flanders has been spending here lately? I mean, it was great to see him at Gary's party, but I don't think he's been around the shop this much in a decade. He spends most of his time with Charlie and the rest of it walking the floor talking with the teams. I wonder if he's saying goodbye to everyone."

"I don't know Kelli, I just don't know," replied Jack.

He just shook his head at the thought of losing the steady hand of the Flanders family and looked back at the charts and graphs laid out on his desk. Kelli took this as her cue to leave and turned and walked out of Jack's office and toward the cafeteria, still twirling her hair and making gum cracking sounds.

Jack was gathering up the colorful charts and graphs, still trying to figure out how he was going to keep the shop floor teams engaged when there was a knock on his door frame. He turned to see Dean Berzani standing in his open doorway. He hadn't talked to Dean, other than to apologize, since he had him pressed up against Veronica Appleton's wall, the day Gary Peterson was walked out of the plant. Jack looked at Dean a few long moments, wondering what this visit was all about.

"Uh, Jack," began Dean, looking furtively around the larger office area, "do you got a minute?"

"Sure Dean, come in," said Jack.

Dean walked into Jack's office and proceeded to shut the door behind him and close the aluminum shades so that anybody looking would see only the closed door. This piqued Jack's interest in this unannounced visit, especially since Dean hadn't been at the Amalgamated facility since Gary's dismissal, instead opting to stay back at Shiloh and run Continuous Improvement from the safety of his own office. Dean dropped down into one of the chairs in front of

Jack's desk and sat silently for a full minute. Jack sat back in his chair and waited for Dean to announce the purpose of this get-together. Jack was finally going to ask Dean what this was all about when Dean finally took a deep breath, set his shoulders back, and looked squarely at Jack. Jack simply stared back at Dean, his face betraying nothing.

"Look Jack," began Dean, "I owe you an apology."

"For?" asked Jack, now wary of what was coming next.

"Whaddya mean 'for?' said Dean, "for everything. For being a complete ass to you and your team. For terrorizing Thanh. For Gary. For dissing what you and your team have built here."

"So you *do* know his name," said Jack with equal parts curiosity and wariness. Where was this going and what brought this on?

"Yeah, I know his name," continued Dean, "but you gotta understand something here Jack, I have been a fish completely out of water here ever since the merger. I was born and raised over at Shiloh; it's the only place I've ever worked. I scratched my way from drill press operator up through the ranks until I landed the CI manager job."

"So that gives you license, in your mind, to do *what*?" asked Jack.

"No, Jack, you got it wrong. You got me wrong," continued Dean, now speaking more quietly, without his usual bluster, "At Shiloh, it's all about havin' the sharpest knife and being willing to use it. Publicly and frequently. The place is full of really smart people, but they're all out to make a name for themselves, even if they've gotta stick their shiny knife in your back. Or your face. The bigger the crowd the better. The leadership staff meetings are all about proving you're smarter than everybody else in the room. You get big points if you can catch somebody making a mistake. Or getting a number wrong."

Jack looked at Dean, and began to wonder what it would be like to work in an environment like that. Spending your days worried that somebody was going to snipe at you during a review or a meeting, always looking over your shoulder in an environment of little or no trust. Jack was happy to leave a lot of that behind him when he joined Amalgamated. Still, he thought, that didn't simply make everything that had happened over the last five months 'ok' by any stretch of the imagination.

"So," said Jack, "it sounds pretty ruthless over there. Kelli gave us a bit of feedback when she came over for a week a few months back."

"Yeah," said Dean, "I remember that. We were in a report out and she kept asking questions that you just don't ask over there. I was happy to keep handing her the rope she was gonna hang herself with. The managers all had a good laugh after she left."

"So you didn't give her any help at all then?" asked Jack, leveling his gaze at Dean. Dean look at Jack for a few moments, then closed his eyes and silently shook his head.

"No," said Dean flatly, "I figured that once she left, we'd just keep on keeping on. She was coming back here so she'd be fine. But," he continued, "that was my first taste of this whole 'family' thing at Amalgamated. I thought it was a bunch of crap at first, you know, just something that HR puts up on banners and posters in the locker rooms. But the more time I spent here the more it hit me that this place was different than what I was used to at Shiloh. In fact, it was the exact opposite of what I was used to at Shiloh. I thought Charlie was going to kill me that day out on the floor."

"I thought he was too," said Jack, now smiling at the memory of Dean almost running down the main aisle after Charlie let him know that it was completely unacceptable to behave the way he was.

"Anyway," Dean went on, "that's why I'm here today. I wanna put all that garbage behind us and try and start fresh between us. As equals. None of this 'support team' crap. Can we do that?"

Jack leaned back in his chair and thought about everything Dean had told him. It must have taken a tremendous effort on Dean's part to come here and have this talk. It would be far easier just to sit back at Shiloh and keep churning out audits, charts, metrics, and e-mails around incomplete items.

"Isn't this," Jack finally said, "going to hurt your standing back at Shiloh? Aren't you going to be joining the 'leper colony' as it were?"

Dean smiled at Jack's comment and shook his head.

"No," Dean said, "I'm not worried about that. I'm kind of on the 'outs' with the leadership team as it is anyways."

"Oh," said Jack, raising an eyebrow and again wary of this conversation, "how so?"

"Well," continued Dean, "to be honest, once the beanies got to running through Shiloh's books, what with the IPO coming, they decided that most of the 'savings' that we were booking with the 'blast' events hadn't been realized, so they basically zeroed out that account. Once a few million bucks got zapped from Shiloh's valuation models, I had a 'fall from grace' as it were."

Jack had wondered how all of that dual bookkeeping would end after Kelli gave him and the team the rundown on what was happening at Shiloh. So, once Dean had lost his 'value' to Steve Bucholtz, he was cast aside. Nice. Great value on the people side of the business, thought Jack. He began unconsciously shaking his head at the thought of it all. And why, he wondered, did the rest of the world think that a merger between Shiloh and Amalgamated was such a fantastic idea? Probably, he mused, because the outside world, the financial world especially, has no knowledge of, nor care for, the impacts of a company's culture. To them it was just a numbers thing. People didn't exist; they were just cost walking on two legs.

"So that's a no?" asked Dean, shaking Jack from his thoughts.

"What?" said Jack, "no, of course not Dean. I'm sorry, I was just thinking about everything that has led us here. I accept your apology and look forward to working with you going forward in whatever way we can figure out, given the environment here and especially with the madness of the impending IPO."

"Great!" said Dean, "then you're gonna clear it with everybody here. Fantastic!" Dean clapped his hands together and began rubbing them like he was trying to get a genie to come out of a bottle.

"No, Dean," interrupted Jack, "I'm not going to clear anything with anybody."

"What? Why?" asked Dean, a worried look on his face. "I thought you said we were square, you and me."

"*We* are," continued Jack, "but you need to square it with the rest of this place yourself, Dean, you dug these holes and you need to get yourself out of them. I'd suggest you start with Thanh. If anybody asks my opinion, I'll tell them to give you a chance."

Dean chewed his lower lip for a bit and finally looked back at Jack with a grin.

"Done," said Dean, now in a more upbeat mood, "and you're right, Jack, I did this myself and I can fix it. I'll talk with Thanh right away. You got a recommended order I should talk to people here, since you've been the one dealing with the fallout every time I come here?"

"I'd say start with Thanh," said Jack, "and then go to Kelli next. If she doesn't kill you for whatever reason, I'd suggest going to Charlie after that. If you can win Kelli, Charlie will cut you a little more slack. Then you can work your way through the rest of the teams here."

"Kelli huh?" said Dean, rubbing his chin, "you really think the squirt's going to try and kill me?"

"Yes," said Jack, "especially if you call her 'squirt,' so I'd drop that little nickname in a hurry if I were you."

"Old habits," said Dean nodding, "sorry."

"Habits can be changed Dean, you just have to work at them. Every day."

"True enough Jack, true enough," said Dean as he got up and extended his hand over Jack's desk. Jack stood up and accepted the handshake, a handshake that hopefully meant the beginning of a better relationship between Jack's team and the team over at Shiloh. Dean turned and walked over to Jack's door, where he paused and turned back to Jack.

"Jack," Dean asked, "do you want this open or shut?"

"Open," said Jack, "we don't like to have our doors shut if we don't have to. Old habits." Jack smiled.

With that, Dean walked out of Jack's office and over to where Thanh was busily working away, automating the corporate 'requirements' for data reporting and charting. Jack could see Dean talking to Thanh and wondering exactly how he was going to apologize for treating Thanh so harshly. Thanh, to Jack's surprise, had quite a lot to say to Dean who, at several times during the conversation, held his hands up, palms out, as if to say 'hey, I get it.' Thanh's forwardness was probably due to Kelli's influence, Jack thought, smiling. Finally, after about five minutes Thanh stood and extended his hand to Dean, who took it and shook it with both hands. Dean's smile was ear to ear and, Jack thought, it looks earnest. That's something new for Dean, let's hope it lasts.

After agreeing to start over with Thanh, Dean found Kelli out on the floor and began his mea culpa speech with her. Jack had guessed right, in that Kelli sought nothing more than Dean's painful, protracted, agonizing, televised and web-streamed demise, first threatening to stuff him into the cardboard crusher and then changing her mind and deciding to strap him to a log and run him through the sawmill a few times, all in the name of 'chlorinating the gene pool.' Dean's persistence, however, finally got a grudging acceptance that Kelli would put him on 'double secret probation,' and maintaining the right, at any time, to run him through the sawmill; no questions asked. Thus began Dean's journey of penance and reflection, which would last the better part of a month.

* * *

The financial world received another shock two weeks later, as it was announced that the impending IPO of the newly merged Amalgamated and Shiloh was put on hold 'indefinitely.' For the next week the various financial bobble heads traded their inane theories as to why the IPO had been shelved. Was it a Chinese takeover? Were they being sued? Had Zack Flanders really died?

The true reason for the 'indefinite hold' was that the private equity group that owned ten percent of the newly merged company had found a buyer for its ownership share at a price well above what the IPO was going to give them. The return on the private equity's investment was close to thirty percent, which would give them an annualized return of close to fifty percent, which they all agreed was a brilliant move on their part. They took the offer without even consulting Amalgamated or Shiloh, which was their right, they said, based on the fine print in the merger documents. The generous buyer of their ownership share was a recently formed Delaware LLC, which no-one had ever heard of. Once the financial media began digging into the ownership of the buyer, they found that the LLC was majority-owned by one Zachary Flanders.

The talking heads on the financial news networks were apoplectic and began a blizzard of speculation on how Zack was able to form and capitalize the new LLC to a degree that it was able to buy out the private equity's stake on the new firm. Flanders must have, they guessed, sold or mortgaged everything that the Flanders family owned, and then some. He probably had to hock his new grand baby, they surmised.

In truth, Zack had done exactly that, minus the grand baby, plus he went to his suppliers, most having been with Amalgamated since its beginnings almost a century prior, and had received access to even more lines of credit at very reasonable rates. It turns out that the suppliers weren't very happy with the unilateral price reductions, which in some cases made them run at a loss, and doubling of payment terms, which put them into a cash flow crunch. In their estimation it was a smarter move to have a Flanders in control of the company than to keep getting hammered on costs and terms. When the dust settled, Zachary Flanders now controlled fifty five percent of the merged company, mostly because the private equity firm wouldn't take less than a full buyout of their share.

Zachary Flanders held town hall meetings at both facilities to outline his vision going forward.

Kelli was reportedly seen out on the floor leading Business Unit 3 in the Macarena. She hotly denied the accusation until the cell phone videos began popping up. Her reply was only that 'it was making a comeback.'

```
TDSTMP:    092315.0800Z
PRTY:      STANDARD

SNDR:      KOROMO BASE

TRGT:      GHQ

SITREP:    RECONSTRUCTION OF KOROMO
           BASE CONTINUES. RESUPPLY OF
           AMMUNITION AND SUPPLIES
           NEARING COMPLETION. REGULAR
           PATROLS ARE NEARING
           DESTROYED FIREBASES TO
           ASSESS. REINFORCEMENTS
           DEPLOYED IN ALL AREAS.

[END TRANSMISSION]
```

Chapter 13

September 23, 2015

Jack pushed open the door leading to the cafeteria and set his safety glasses up on top of his head. Behind him walked Charlie and Kelli, who were deep in conversation. Jack poured himself a cup of coffee into his battered mug and headed to the cash register to pay. He was glad to see Mary behind the cash register, gave her a big smile and handed her a dollar bill from his wallet. He stood over by the vending machines and waited for Charlie and Kelli to pay and walk over. Jack was still feeling a bit under the weather, having suffered a severe bout of stomach flu over the last two weeks. His doctor told him that it was 'going around' and had him trying to rehydrate after suffering miserably.

Unfortunately for Jack, it had also cost him a trip with Charlie, Geoff Mueller, Pete Valensky, and Kelli across the state to Tri-Star Fabrication, where the five of them were supposed to attend a three-day workshop on something called the Improvement Kata and Coaching Kata. Jack's sudden illness kept him from going, but Kelli promised to take good notes. Jack knew that Kelli never took notes, but having her there would go a long way in getting him at least familiar with the training until he could go and participate himself. Jack took another sip of coffee and felt his stomach rumbling in protest. Maybe the coffee wasn't his most brilliant idea.

"Hey Charlie, Kelli," said Jack as they walked up, "how did the training go last week?"

"Morning Jack," answered Charlie, "you feeling any better? That flu bug can be nasty."

"Tell me about it," said Jack, "and yeah, I'm feeling a lot better today. I think we're out in front of it. I just need to lay off any spicy or overly sweet stuff for a little while longer."

"Then big boss-man," said Kelli with a smile, "I won't offer you a sip of my triple, venti, half sweet, non-fat, caramel macchiato." She waved her cup in the general direction of Jack's nose. He felt his stomach gurgle again in protest, and turned his head away while making a contorted face.

"Kelli," Jack protested, "how do you drink that stuff and stay so skinny?"

"Awesome genes, I guess," she responded, still smiling.

"Glad to hear it," said Jack, still eyeing her cup warily. "But I really want to hear about how the training went. While you guys were across the state and I was never more than ten feet from my bathroom, I had a copy of the book Toyota Kata, by Mike Rother, delivered to my house so I could try and figure out what you were doing."

"Jack, I gotta tell you," said Charlie, "I was a bit skeptical about what we were going to be doing, but in the end I think it went really well. I think you're going to like this approach to CI. Given how little notice before this trip we got from Zack, after his little coup here at Amalgamated, I wasn't real thrilled, but hey, he's our owner again, so I saluted the flag and took Geoff, Pete, and short round with me."

"Yeah," said Jack, "I still can't believe what Zack Flanders did to get Amalgamated back. The Shiloh team must've been in complete shock when the announcement came out."

"They were," offered Charlie, "and Zack had me come with him as he was making the announcements. Steve Bucholtz, their VP of Manufacturing, about fell out of his throne when Zack broke the news. And I thought that the Appleton woman was going to cry. Seems they had already come up with lots of ways to spend the money they were planning to make on the IPO. I doubt they were planning on sticking around too long after it happened, judging by their responses. Bucholtz announce he was leaving the next day."

"Wish I could've been there," said Kelli as she took a sip of her caffeine-based coffee creation.

"Now, now," said Charlie, "it wasn't a time to gloat or try and settle any scores." Charlie looked down at Kelli with a serious face and held her gaze a few long seconds. He then smiled broadly and gave her a wink. "But, I must admit, I've had *worse* days around here."

"Hah, I bet you have!" Kelli snorted.

"Anyway," said Jack, "how was this training event you went to? What went on?"

"Tri-Star was great," said Kelli, "they were a good operation and they had a pretty switched on leadership team. Zack Flanders, it turns out, sits on their board, so he knew the event was happening. That's why he tried to get us in on such short notice."

"Tell him about your new heartthrob short round," prodded Charlie with a grin.

"Ah, Tony," said Kelli wistfully, "The future Mr. O'Malley." She stopped talking and stared at something far in the distance, with a soft smile playing across her face. Jack stared at her for a few moments, waiting for her to go on. When she didn't, he helpfully cleared his throat.

"Hmm? Oh, yes, the training, right," Kelli said, now rejoining the conversation. "The training was led by a consultant named Tony McAllister, and he was *dreamy*." Kelli stopped for a moment, but began again when she saw Jack growing a little impatient. "We had a little bit of classroom discussion around the basic concepts and then we spent most of our time on the floor."

"Dreamy?" asked Jack, arching an eyebrow.

"He's not from around here Jack," offered Charlie. "He's Australian and I think little Miss Kelli here just loved listening to him talk. You know, with that Australian accent." Charlie was now grinning at the memory.

"Ah," said Jack, "now things are beginning to come into focus."

"Trouble was," continued Charlie, "I couldn't understand him half the time. He was using some kind of slang and I had to stop him more than once. Smart guy though."

"I don't care if he just read from the phone book," said Kelli, "as long as I got to hear that beautiful accent."

"Ok, fine," said Jack, "but what did you guys do for the three days?"

"First," said Charlie, "we talked a little bit about what we were trying to learn about this whole Improvement Kata and Coaching Kata idea. We talked a bit about how people don't spend any time trying to think scientifically anymore and we don't learn anything new. And yet we somehow think we can be better problem solvers doing things the same old, haphazard way. Made sense."

"Interesting," said Jack, "that's what I read in the Kata book as well. The whole 'jumping to conclusions' and 'my way or the highway' mentality is short-circuiting our ability to solve problems." I understand 'kata' is used in the martial arts to mean a routine that you learn through repeated practice and the big kahuna black belt watches until you do it exactly as he showed you. Follow the kata or you'll practice the routine forever. Practicing the kata everyday breaks old habits and begins to change the way we think about problems.

"Bingo," agreed Charlie, "we spend all our time arguing about whose idea or approach is best and then fighting for control of how things get done. Instead, we should be arguing about what we should try next, on our way to the Challenge."

"The Challenge, boss-man" added Kelli, "is our starting point. It's the first thing we establish. It's something that's critical to our success over the long term. It's not something that's going to be delivered over the next thirty days or so. This can be something that takes three years to achieve. Or more. It truly is a *Challenge*."

"Exactly," added Charlie, "it's how we get the troops aligned and keep everybody focused on the way we're heading. It's like you told me before Jack, about how we need to keep people focused on a goal and not running around mindlessly 'eliminating waste' thinking they're doing the right thing."

"That sounds like a solid approach," said Jack, "so once the Challenge was established, then what did you do over at Tri-Star?"

"First," said Kelli, "we had to do something called 'Grasping the Current Condition.' This wasn't anything mystical or secret; it was a very common sense approach. We created a Current State Map and gathered all of the relevant data and populated the map. We then worked with the Tri-Star leadership team and created the Future State Map, which had our first challenge embedded in it."

"How so?" asked Jack.

"Quality and Delivery," said Charlie, "these guys could make stuff cheaply, but they were struggling with customer returns and on-time delivery. The Future State called these out specifically and the leadership team set an aggressive Challenge to the teams based on the mapping exercise."

"Yeah," said Kelli, "it was a bit of a shock to the teams, and there was a bit of panic at first, but they calmed down when the leadership team talked about the process and the support they were going to get."

"The leadership team explained that nobody was expected to reach the Challenge in one big, risky leap. It would be done through small steps and experimentation," continued Charlie. "Once the Current Condition was identified, the team spent some time figuring out their First Target Condition."

"Their first target eh?" said Jack.

"No, Jack," said Charlie, "not simply a target, but a target *condition*. Not just the results of the line, but how the line was going to run, the patterns and processes that would be in place that gave the output results. Once the teams were done with this, they were able to identify what the gaps were; the obstacles, and then they were ready to move forward."

"Except for the First Target Condition thing, that approach sounds pretty similar to what we were doing here," said Jack, "so what was the big difference?"

"The biggest difference Jack," said Charlie as he took a sip of his coffee, "is that instead of trying to implement a typical action plan, like we were doing here, the focus was on the teams running small experiments, frequently, to overcome obstacles that they identified."

"Obstacles," said Jack.

"Yep," added Kelli, "*obstacles* to the First Target Condition. The teams didn't know what to do first, so they listed all of the obstacles they could think of that would keep them from achieving their First Target Condition. These obstacles were just outside of their Threshold of Knowledge."

"Say again," said Jack.

"Threshold of Knowledge Jack," said Charlie, "it's everything we know about a process and no more. If our threshold were farther out, we'd be performing better already. We need to run these little experiments to expand our knowledge of the processes, overcome obstacles one by one, and keep marching toward the Challenge."

"Sounds like," said Jack, "a great name for a rock band. The *Threshold of Knowledge.*"

Kelli just rolled her eyes at Jack's longest running joke between the two. Any curious or funny phrase was instantly turned into the name of a mythical rock band. Jack had been doing this back during the launch he and Kelli were on. Charlie just looked at Jack and arched an eyebrow.

"Anyway, bad puns aside," Kelli went on, "once the actual teams on the floor identified their obstacles, then we began to design an experiment to tackle the specific obstacle."

"Didn't the teams," asked Jack, "want to do more than simply tackle one obstacle at a time? Surely they had the bandwidth to get a lot more done during that time, didn't they?"

"Probably," said Charlie, "but the whole point was to get the teams thinking more scientifically, rather than shotgun blasting the area with action plan items and hoping for the best when it came to the results. The teams were going to be practicing the mindset of predicting what would happen, running the experiment, and seeing what happened. If the experiment was successful, they had a new current condition. If not, they got smarter because they just learned something they didn't know before and came up with another experiment based on what they just learned."

"When you say 'practicing the mindset' Charlie," said Jack, "you're saying that the goal wasn't to achieve the improvements, but rather to develop habits. Is that right?"

"Right again Jack," said Charlie, "the goal of the Improvement Kata isn't to deliver some result on some project with some kind of 'return on investment,' but rather to teach the teams a method of practicing that will help them be better problem solvers. I really like this approach Jack, I gotta admit."

"That jibes with what I read," said Jack, "about kata being structured routines to help people develop new skills."

"Just like," said Kelli, "when you take your golf lessons. Same concept, only this is in the business world and not on some golf course with you scaring the squirrels half to death every time you address the ball." This reference to Jack's meager golf game earned Kelli a frown and stare from Jack. Kelli just gave Jack her sweetest smile and continued.

"The teams would do these practice routines every day to try and strengthen their mental muscles. It was very structured," she said.

"How structured?" asked Jack.

"Our coach, Tony," said Charlie, "would come out every day around the end of the shift and review with us the same things. The *exact* same things. Every day. He had a small card in his shop floor jacket that he pulled out and used as a script. I doubt he needed it, but he was also trying to show us how the Coaching Kata worked."

"So you were learning," said Jack, "and Tony was teaching you the Improvement Kata and you got to see him doing the Coaching Kata routines as well."

"Yep," said Kelli, "because we're going to be working as coaches, eventually, so we needed to see that as well. Plus, we got to listen to Tony talk." Kelli's vision began to blur a bit as her gaze began to drift beyond the current conversation. Charlie shook his head and chuckled.

"Stay focused short round," Charlie said, "Jack, Tony would ask us every day to explain our target and actual conditions, to make sure we knew our gaps. He'd ask us what the last thing we tried was, and what happened. Did we get what we expected to get, you know? What did we learn? And what were we going to try next and when should he come back and see how we did? It never changed. And pretty quickly, we knew what he was going to ask, so we made sure we knew what we were doing and the followed the same script. It was pretty powerful stuff. It kept the teams focused and everybody thinking about the same thing."

"Where did you guys meet?" asked Jack. "Did Tri-Star set aside some space where you could all get together?"

"Nope," answered Kelli, "we set up our Learner's Storyboard right next to their production control board and had our daily meetings there."

"Ah yes," said Jack, "I remember that part from the book. Everything was on the same board; the Challenge, Current and Target conditions, Obstacles, and the PDCA Record of experiments."

"Exactly," offered Charlie, "so we'd meet there every day and recap what we had done and what we were going to try next."

"Was there," asked Jack, "any pushback about the Learner's Storyboard being manual? You know the usual complaint about being able to spread best practices digitally and all that?"

"No need to worry about that," said Charlie, "because this isn't something you can copy and tell other people 'do this.' Think about it. Each experiment is for a specific obstacle on a specific process in a specific environment, internal and external. What are the odds that somebody else can just blindly replicate what one team is doing? Zero, that's the odds. Besides, if somebody's interested, they can come out to a Learner's Storyboard and see for themselves and talk to the teams, can't they?"

"I'm with you Charlie," said Jack, "and I'm glad you're so interested in this."

"I'd better be Jack," said Charlie, "because Zack needs us to set some pretty aggressive Challenges both here and at Shiloh over the next few years. The man's got some serious debts to pay back."

"Are you," asked Jack, "going to start with this approach over at Shiloh as well?"

"Nope," said Charlie, "no way. We don't have any coaches other than Tony at the moment, and we're not going to let this get out of hand. We're going to focus on developing the skills and coaches here and then expand as soon as we can."

"See boss man," offered Kelli, "an old dog *can* learn new tricks." Kelli smiled up at Charlie as she took another sip of her sugary, caffeinated beverage.

"Awright short round," said Charlie, "I suppose I had that coming. See Jack, early in the training I wanted to know how fast we could spread this through the organization, knowing the challenges we had ahead of us as a group. Once we talked it through, it made sense that once we had people trained up on the coaching part of this, then and only then would we expand what we were doing. That approach makes sense to me as I don't want our guys and girls running around without the skills needed to make this a success. Tony talked about a 'chain of coaching' when it came to these kata routines."

"A chain of coaching," parroted Jack.

"Yeah Jack," said Kelli, "think of it like a chain of people from our front-line value-adders all the way up to Jolly Green here. Depending on where you are on the chain, you could be the person doing the improvement routines, or you could be in the coaching role. For everybody except the front-liners, you'll be doing both roles. Sometimes you'll be coaching your team and sometimes you'll be getting coached by your boss. So we're going to need some training and practice at being a coach. Some of us will need more training that others, of course." Kelli elbowed Charlie in the ribs, which is as high as her elbow could reach.

"Right, right," said Charlie, smiling at Kelli, "don't you worry about me short round, I'll do just fine."

"So where do we go from here?" asked Jack.

"Well," answered Charlie, "we've got about two weeks to work on getting our Challenges straightened around and get working on our Current Conditions before Tony can be on deck. Zack has worked it out to have Tony here regularly to help us get started. We're going to be the advance group here, with Geoff, Stan and me working on our team in Business Unit Six and you, short round, and your group supporting Business Unit Eight."

"Why," asked Jack, "are you moving over to BU 6 instead of staying in the areas where we're already working?"

"Let's face it Jack," said Charlie, "we've got to get those groups back on an even keel after all of the Shiloh shenanigans for the last few months. Those people are a little tired at the moment of the whole 'continuous improvement' thing, so we're going to let them stabilize a little bit, take down all of that garbage wallpapering their areas, and catch their breath before we come back to them with these new routines."

"Sounds fair," said Jack as he thought of all of the 'global best practice' indicators that they had been busily automating and hanging all over the production floor. Kelli and Thanh had been working tirelessly to automate these charts as much as possible, but there was considerable unhappiness with the entire process, with the teams near open rebellion over the myriad indicators and audits that they now were performing under Shiloh's system.

Thankfully the 'friendly' takeover by Zack Flanders had brought that to a halt. The teams now were working on doing what Jack had dubbed the 'one S,' meaning the first step of the 5S process of 'sorting.' This had the teams removing all unnecessary clutter from their areas, focusing on all of the multi-color charts and additional boards that had been set up around the shop.

"Two weeks until Tony gets here," said Kelli, "how will I ever stand it?"

"You'll survive, short round," said Charlie as he began walking away from Jack and Kelli, "so if you'll excuse me you two, I've got to talk to Geoff Mueller about some particularly *challenging* items, if you catch my drift."

Kelli rolled her eyes at the pun and Jack simply smiled, his stomach gurgling once in agreement.

```
TDSTMP:    101215.1200Z
PRTY:      STANDARD

SNDR:      KOROMO BASE

TRGT:      GHQ

SITREP:    KOROMO BASE RECONSTRUCTION
           COMPLETE. INTELLIGENCE
           OPERATIVE HAS ARRIVED AND
           IS BRIEFING THE SQUADS.
           PATROLS ARE OUT ON
           SCHEDULE. FIREBASES ARE
           OCCUPIED AND RESUPPLY
           COMMENCING.

[END TRANSMISSION]
```

Chapter 14

October 12, 2015

The sun was just rising to the east, bathing the conference room in its warm glow as Jack stood motionless, watching the miracle of nature slowly change the color palette from indigo to a deep burgundy, with the high clouds now showing a crimson strip just beginning to form on their undersides. It felt appropriate to Jack, and analogous to his journey here at Amalgamated.

When Kelli persuaded him to join the team here, he brought with him all of the experiences and knowledge that he had gained throughout almost thirty years in the field. Continuous Improvement had evolved quite a bit over the decades since the 'west' first took steps to learning what their competitors in the 'east' were doing so well. The first craze was that of 'Kaizen,' heralded by Imai's book back in the early 1980's that had office people gluing pencil nubs together to help improve the fortunes of their respective businesses.

When that failed to yield the results necessary, a massive undertaking began to grasp the specific tools that were implemented throughout the world-class factories. Hordes of consultants began hawking packages that were guaranteed to 'make you Lean' or to 'Lean out your operations.' Jack smiled at his early memories in the trenches as company after company would try and deploy some sort of 'stairway to heaven' roll-out methodology, as he liked to call it, whereby the company was given a first, easy, set of tools to master and deploy. Once they passed a rigorous audit, usually done by the consultants, they were deemed 'ready' to progress to the next level, where they would again have to master a toolset and be judged on their level of deployment.

The original teachings of the Japanese consultants that came to the U.S. to help with the transformation became diluted, mistranslated, or simply ignored. We didn't want to hear, Jack thought, about a *journey*, nor did we want to put in the hard work required to effect a deep culture change. We wanted it quick, cheap, and dirty, like a project: a beginning, gather resources, attack the problem, declare victory, and take the team photo. Smiles everybody!

The silly things we did back then, Jack thought, as he slowly took a sip of coffee, careful not to move too fast or the room's motion detector would blind him as it clicked on the overhead fluorescent lights. We were running around the facility labeling everything that didn't move, all in the name of Visual Management. Jack shook his head slowly at the thought of all of the garbage cans, light switches, water fountains, doors, cabinets, staplers, and who knows what else that got a label dutifully stuck to them as part of the deployment process. One facility he worked in actually failed a consultant-led audit because, in their words, the factory wasn't 'visual enough.' When it was pointed out to the consultants by the plant leadership that 'being visual' didn't seem to have anything to do with 'being profitable,' which was where the consultants' fees were coming from, the facility was promptly given a passing grade, but put on 'probation.'

The years went by and various outside groups found a lucrative business model in 'certifying' people and facilities. The focus then became on how to get the coveted certification. Entire staffs were dedicated to dissecting the evaluation criteria and putting together mini-task forces to ensure compliance and a favorable outcome during the certification visit. Once that magical 'certification' was achieved, in most cases, the teams were disbanded, the plaque was given a place of honor in the main lobby, and people went back to doing their real work. Without fail, within a year or so the performance of the facility began to slip back to where it was before the certification efforts began, and before long the U.S. was dotted with poorly performing factories all proudly displaying their 'certification' from the various, self-proclaimed arbiters of all things Lean.

Within all of this mechanized, consultant-led, metric-driven, mass deployment was another, smaller movement; one that focused on the importance of learning, effective training, coaching, and people development. This type of deployment spread more slowly, constrained by the availability of truly effective, capable coaches. It also failed to gain traction with the various leadership teams that didn't have the patience or understanding to lead the development of their teams; they had quarterly expectations to manage and bonuses to protect. This approach was called 'organic' versus the truly 'mechanistic' approach in much wider use.

Jack had found himself drawn more to the organic focus on people development, but he was pragmatic enough to know that the business had to be moving in the right direction in order to sustain the efforts. He had comfortably settled upon using the Pilot Line approach to launch his transformation efforts. By creating a little 'laboratory' within a facility, all of his teams' efforts could be narrowly focused and everything was contained within a single process or business unit. This approach had been proven time and time again in Jack's experience. The biggest challenge was always to ensure that the people in the area had intensive, one-on-one coaching throughout the transformation so they developed the skills and understanding to both sustain the improved processes and continue on their own journey to excellence.

The drawback of course, was that this deep development of people greatly slowed the ability of the team to spread across an organization. On the other hand he couldn't imagine any another approach that developed deep learning so that when the team eventually began to disengage, what was left in its wake was effective and sustainable. So the perennial battle was always speed of deployment versus sustainability; could the teams spend enough time training and developing the local teams to support and continue to improve the processes, with the deployment teams acting as coaches? Now we're using this new approach to develop skills, the Improvement Kata and Coaching Kata. The idea is that through structured practice routines we'll develop the right way of thinking and acting to improve toward a challenge. Fake it until we make it. Act your way into a new way of thinking versus the other way around, which, in Jack's opinion, was where too many companies' efforts failed. They wanted to think their way to action. Bad idea.

All of these thoughts ran though Jack's mind as he watched the clouds go from crimson to orange, to a brilliant yellow, and finally fade to white as the sun broke the horizon behind the massive expanse of trees at the edge of the property. This was a beautiful place, Jack thought, happy that no one had chosen to repurpose the conference room or turn it into an office. Thankfully the space that Steve Bucholtz, the ex-VP had chosen, was closer to the parking lot and less of a walk. Jack slowly took another sip of coffee, battling with the motion sensor to keep the lights off a bit longer, when he heard footsteps coming down the hallway. Ah well, he thought, it was a nice break while it lasted.

Moments later he heard the door handle turn and the door opened into the conference room, the overhead fluorescent lights snapping on as the motion sensor detected the opening of the conference room door, bathing the room in their harsh, white glare. Jack turned to see Tony McAllister standing there with his genial, yet dry grin.

"G'day Jack, how ya goin' mate?" said Tony in his thick Australia accent. Jack couldn't help but smile, as he understood Kelli's fascination with Tony. He had never had the chance to work closely with anybody from the famous land down under. Tony had come to Amalgamated shortly after Zack Flanders bought back a controlling interest and was going to be there full time for at least the next six months or so. They were trying to get him for a year. Tony was a veteran of the vaunted Toyota Motor Corporation and had been an internal trainer, which at Toyota meant you were considered at the very top of the class in terms of skills and abilities. Jack knew that Amalgamated had been very fortunate to get Tony dedicated to them for such a long stretch.

Tony was being brought in to help begin the deployment of the Improvement Kata approach to skill development that Jack had read and heard so much about. He read enough to know that it was not an approach that Toyota used, but rather was developed by thought leader Mike Rother to address a gap in the way companies outside Toyota approached people development. In Toyota there were many coaches like Tony who had the advanced coaching ability to develop in others the skills for continuous improvement. In other companies... not so much. Toyota Kata was based on a structured approach to scientific thinking and practice routines so less experienced coaches could teach learners the skills to work toward challenging goals that at first seem impossible. Tony had been exposed to the approach long after leaving Toyota, but took to it naturally and agreed it did a good job of developing the skills many of his associates at Toyota learned from seasoned veteran coaches over the span of many years.

The team took to Tony and his laid back style quickly, with Thanh and Kelli dueling to see who could look up the fastest what some of Tony's more colorful turns of phrase in Aussie slang meant. Tony would be in the office and mention something about 'having to hop on the blowa for a tick' and Thanh and Kelli would furiously type as they tried to discern what he meant. The score was pretty even, with Kelli having a one or two point lead over Thanh. Tony was amused by the whole production and did his best to keep Kelli and Thanh busy researching the furthest reaches of Australian slang.

"I'm fine Tony," said Jack, still looking out at the sunrise, with the sun just starting to break above the tree line, highlighting the red, yellow, and orange leaves. Tony walked up and stood next to Jack and looked out the window. "I always like coming here if I need a chance to think, away from the distractions of the office, or the needs of the floor."

"I can see why mate," said Tony, looking at the oak and maple trees at the edge of the property seem to be catching fire from the bright morning sun, "this view is a bloody rippah." Tony stood for a few moments more, enjoying the little fireworks show from Mother Nature before he turned to Jack. "So, Jack, how are you gettin' along with your training group?" Once Tony had come on board, Jack immediately joined Business Unit Six as they began to learn the Improvement Kata.

"We're doing well, I think," said Jack, "once the team got their Challenge from the Pete, the business unit supervisor, we set to work defining the Current Condition, which had a few bumps, but went pretty well, overall. We talked a bit as a team about the concept of the 'nested challenge,' where challenges at Charlie's level are distilled down through the organization and become relevant to each group. Charlie's go to Geoff, who then works to get them to his supervisors, like Pete, and then to the team level, where I'm learning."

"What kind of bumps are you talking about?" asked Tony, even though he already knew the answer.

"Getting some of the information on the process itself was a challenge," answered Jack, "because we didn't have very good shop floor systems to capture anything meaningful. The team had plenty of output metrics, like Quality, Safety, and Cost, but we struggled when we tried to go deeper. In our training we were taught to observe many repetitions to observe current operating patterns. As we dug deeper we began to envision measurements systems that would give us a better picture of the how the line operated."

"Yeah, I remember," said Tony, "the team did a great job. I was impressed that you guys got your First Target Condition set and then started getting all of your Obstacles up on your Learner's Storyboard. Some of those, mate, were pretty interesting."

"For sure," said Jack with a smile, "we definitely struggled there a bit. At first we just kept listing outside roadblocks that we couldn't control, like product design, sales, aftermarket, and those kinds of things. Once we got our heads around the real problems, those within our control, then we were able to start putting together a real Obstacles list. Of course you know all this. You were coaching us, so it must have seemed like we were a little dense at that point in the process."

"Not at all mate," said Tony, "it happens all the time. The point is for you and the team to get there with some coaching. Yeah,

I coulda jumped in, suggested Toyota solutions, and then Bob's your uncle, but where the value in that?" Jack inferred that 'Bob's your uncle' was similar to 'voila' and nodded in agreement.

"Well, it worked," said Jack, "and when we got straightened around, the team really went to town getting the Obstacles up on the Parking Lot. But I've got to ask you, now that we're deep into learning both the Improvement Kata and my team and the leadership team are learning the Coaching Kata, isn't there a risk that this is going to take over all of our activities? What happens when people ask about doing a major reengineering on line layouts, or if we still need to use the A3 report when we're working on a problem or a proposal? Are we just going to take the Kata tool and use it to replace everything else?"

"Hold on, stop right there mate," said Tony holding a hand up, "look, here's the deal. The Improvement Kata and Coaching Kata aren't just another lean tool; they're a *way* of doing something. In Japan anyone in the martial arts will know what a kata is. It's how they *learn* the martial arts. The master develops the form and order of a specific body movement. The students practice it over and over until they can do it exactly as the teacher wants. They don't go on until they master the first step and then the next step and finally put them all together. Think of those practice routines as something like a 'starter kata,' where your job is to simply follow your coach's teaching and do exactly what she or he does without deviation. You screw up, you get immediate corrective feedback from the teacher, to make sure you don't develop any bad habits."

"Isn't that," said Jack, "like the part of Job Instruction Training where the trainer is taught to stop the student at the first sign of deviation from the standard? To correct any mistakes as soon as they're detected?"

"Exactly," said Tony, "that's exactly why you do that in JI training. Stop the bad habit from forming. Look, we've been learning and perfecting these methods for thousands of years. It's the basics of learning a craft deeply. In Japan more than other places this approach to skill development is still alive and well. One thing Rother did was study what brain science tells us about skill development. It backs up what we've learned through trial and error. The circuits up here," Tony tapped his temple for effect, "really can be strengthened. Not like a muscle, mind you, but more like an electric circuit that gets more and more insulation around it every time you perform the task correctly." Jack was mentally picturing an exposed copper wire slowly building up layers of insulation around it, ensuring that the circuit would fire without mistake, or any 'leakage' due to gaps in the insulation.

"But," continued Tony, "it's gotta be frequent practice with feedback. Take the bloody aggravating sport of golf. I could go to the driving range and hit a thousand of those little round buggers until me hands bled, and I'd never get any better, because I wouldn't get any feedback as to what I was doing wrong. I'd just keep reinforcing bad habits. Now, give me one of those swing coaches mate, and watch me get better in a hurry. She could see what I was doing wrong, stop me, show me the correct way, maybe even break down the swing into smaller components that I could work on, and then practice putting them together into a proper swing. We'd work on things like grip, stance, balance, address, backswing, shoulder turn, those types of things. Whatever it takes to send that blasted little white ball straight down the fairway. In time, with practice, I'd be improving noticeably. It's not the quantity of practice you do Jack, it's more about the *quality*, and you get the best quality training when you have a dedicated coach that's helping you reach your targets."

"That Rother bloke is clever," Tony said. "He has some pretty good ideas about the core skills people need to improve toward big challenges. When I saw his Improvement Kata model I could relate every step to what my Japanese sensei were teaching me at Toyota. Let me show you how it works. It's quite simple really."

Tony walked over to one of the white boards mounted on the wall, picked up a black dry-erase marker and started drawing up at the top right hand corner of the board. He drew a circle and wrote 'challenge' inside the circle. "You start with a *Challenge*. You would not believe the bloody challenges the Japanese would give me," Tony said as he tapped the white board with the marker.

"Impossible. But I achieved all of them and wasn't sure looking back how I did it."

Tony then drew another circle toward the bottom left corner of the white board and wrote 'Current Condition' inside it. "Then, I wasn't allowed to do anything else, or guess about solutions, until I went to the gemba to understand the current condition. Go and see, go and see, and Tony-san, please go back and see again. Maybe no good Tony-san. Every time I thought I understood they would send me back for more and I would learn some more."

Tony drew another circle on the white board, on an imaginary line connecting the current condition to the challenge. Tony then wrote 'Target Condition' in the circle. "Now was the funny part. I had to set some targets for improvement. But they didn't want big outcomes that I would try to meet in the next year or two. That was already in the Challenge. They wanted me to break down the problem into little pieces, like the way you break down a golf swing. Then they wanted to know what I expected to achieve next, in the next few weeks. Rother calls this a 'Target Condition.' The Japanese never called it that, but it makes sense to me. The target condition is not only an outcome, like percent defects, but also a process characteristic like having in-process checks. So we set the *next* Target Condition, very important, and make sure we know *when* we're going to achieve it. Without that time constraint, this is nothing more than a dream, mate."

Tony then drew a rather haphazard staircase connecting the two circles with some steps looking conventional and some slanting backwards. He then drew a few circles that had frowns and labeled them 'obstacles.' "Then before we can start trying a bunch of ideas for solutions there is one more step—identifying Obstacles." He tapped the dry erase marker on one of the frownie faces. "Now I have to admit this is still a bit of a sore spot for me. In Toyota it was drummed into my head to ask *why* five times until find the root cause. Me trainers would send me back to the gemba over and over

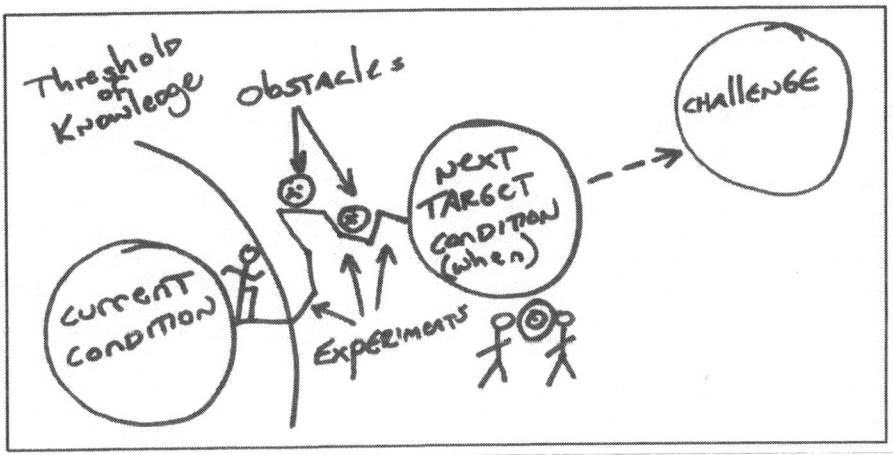

and say 'Tony-san, please, must keep looking, find the root cause!' It was not two or three or four root causes but the one root cause."

"Rother says that we actually don't know what the root cause is, or that there is only one. Instead he says to identify a list of obstacles and write then down in a parking lot. He even says to brainstorm the buggers. Now my Toyota sensei would have my head if I brainstormed root causes, but it makes a certain kind of sense. We really do not know the true root cause by asking why a bunch of times. Now the experienced sensei at Toyota could nail it, the first time. But for novices like me I might have been a bit cocky to think I could find the one true root cause. And experimenting against obstacles will lead you to the root cause anyway, if there really is one."

"Okay, now we get to the good stuff. We start doing. But my sensei would always ask me why I was trying this or that. If I said 'because it's the bloody obvious solution' they would ask 'obvious to whom?' They would then say 'countermeasure, no solution.' This meant in scientific terms it was really a hypothesis. I was theorizing it might bring the process closer to the target condition, but I could not know until I tried. Then they wanted to state out loud what I predicted would happen. Prediction is a big thing at Toyota. They want to know what you expect. Then after the experiment they would want to know what actually happened and finally what did I learn. It was PDCA for every experiment. Tedious, but effective."

"This is built into the Coaching Kata. For every idea you want to try the coach first wants to be reminded of the current condition and target condition to be sure you have thought through how your experiment will move you in the direction of the target condition and then asks these four questions: 'What are you going to test? What do you predict will happen? What happened? What did you learn? Every step is an experiment. This was hammered into my head for years by my sensei, but I never quite thought of it that way." Tony took his Coaching Kata card from his shop coat pocket and tapped it against his forehead to drive home the point.

"So," continued Jack, "in our situation, when we run our experiments, our mini PDCA cycles, we're practicing improvement?"

"Mostly," said Tony, "but what you're really practicing is *thinking* in a scientific way. You're trying to get over an obstacle that's in front of you but you don't know how to get there. You're at the edge of what you know and understand. That's the Threshold of Knowledge. If you can't get beyond that, you're never going to get past that obstacle." Tony took a blue marker from the tray and drew an arc in front of the first obstacle.'

"So we need to minimize the number of times we make a mistake then," said Jack.

"Nah mate, no worries at all," said Tony, "mistakes are fine. Learn from them and don't make them twice. It's not about *not* making mistakes, it's about deepening your understanding of the process and continuing to move forward against that bloody Threshold." Tony tapped the blue arc for effect.

"Some of the team members have been giving me a hard time about the Learner's Storyboard. I know it's the point where we meet to review our progress, but they're complaining it should be done electronically, said Jack."

"Typical," said Tony, "but we need the Storyboard as we continue to develop the practice routines for improvement." He went over to another whiteboard and began to draw out the storyboard. He drew vertical lines and labeled the left section 'next target condition' and the middle section 'current condition,' and finally drew a horizontal line in the right hand portion of the board and labeled the top section 'PDCA cycles' and the lower section 'obstacles.'

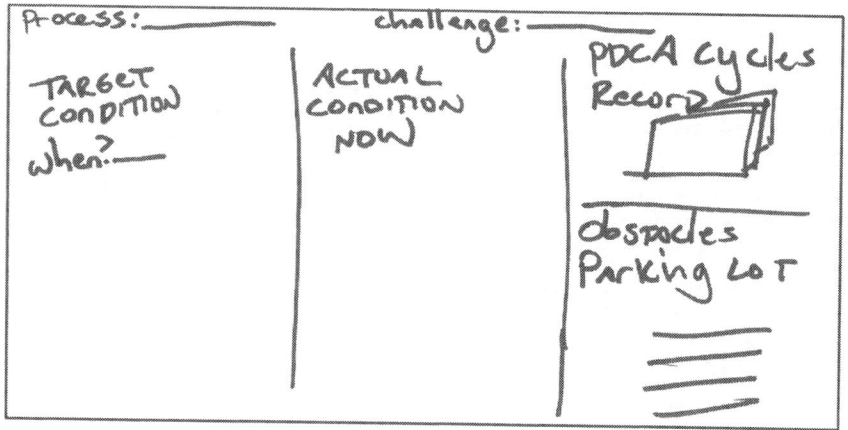

"We keep," continued Tony, "our Current Condition and our Next Target Condition in front of us to keep the teams from going on a 'waste-elimination walkabout,' which benefits nobody. We also force them to think about *when* they're going to be at their Next Target Condition. When people continually focus on where they want to go next and where they are, it makes the discussions much more productive. The teams identify and list their obstacles," Tony tapped the section marked 'Obstacles,' "and then they can conduct their experiments, one PDCA cycle at a time, against a specific Obstacle, improving their understanding of the process and, if it's successful, they move closer to their Next Target Condition. We track each experiment on the PDCA cycles record sheet. These are a bit basic, true, but we need to focus on these starter kata until the teams demonstrate a level of mastery of the basics."

"So when do we get past the starter kata to mastery?" asked Jack.

"Don't worry about that yet," said Tony, "just keep focused on working with the team and get experience with the method and repeat, repeat, repeat. We need to break the old habits of simply doing a bunch of stuff and hoping for the best when the smoke clears. That's the sloppy, easy way, and it leads to backsliding or misunderstanding of cause and effect out on the floor. Won't last mate, so we need to break those mental routines and program ourselves with the new routines. Let those old circuits slowly die off and begin wrapping insulation around the new circuits."

"But," said Jack, "why do you still use the standard question card when you're working with the teams? Surely you've moved beyond the starter kata stage in all of this. Why don't you just come out and work with the teams like the legendary Japanese trainers of old used to?"

"Because mate," said Tony, "I could do that easy, but I need you future coaches to see me using the card and program your brains to use it. No deviations. Maybe at some point in the future you're comfortable enough and have memorized the card well enough to leave it in your pocket. Later you might even get to ask your own questions. The important part is that you don't skip anything and let your teams start deviating from the basic patterns. The card is a simple form of checklist. We want to reinforce the pattern, so we have it on a checklist. Eventually you won't need it, but for now, we'll use it religiously." Tony looked at his watch and then the clock on the wall. "You'd better get going mate, you've got a team meeting in a tick."

Jack looked down at his watch, surprised that he'd been talking to Tony this long. "You're right, thanks. I appreciate the talks on all of this Tony. I know I'm behind the curve a little bit, but once I finish a few more cycles with the team in Business Unit Six as a learner of the Improvement Kata, I'm looking forward to starting the Coaching Kata."

"You'll get there Jack," said Tony, "no worries at all mate. Who knows, in a year or so we might even have you developed all the way to serving as the Second Coach; the Coach's coach."

"Good," said Jack, "I'm really enjoying this whole process. Finally we're doing something that might last beyond management pushing lean down onto everyone."

"Warms me heart Jack," said Tony with a smile, "now can you tell me where there's a terminal up here? I need to hop on the ol' internet and look up some more slang to throw at Kelli and Thanh."

"What?" asked Jack, "I thought you talked like that normally and just toned it down when you and I were talking."

"No way mate," said Tony, "I might be a humble boy from the bush in Bendigo, but I have to spend some time learning the really strange stuff before I lay it on those two. Watching them try and look it up and pretend I don't see them is hilarious. Makes me day. They really struggle with the Far North Queensland stuff."

Jack let that sink in for a minute and couldn't help but smile. "Wow, that's hilarious. And I think there's a guest computer next door in the old Human Resources area. You should be able to find whatever you're looking for."

"Thanks mate," said Tony as he turned to leave, "I might be Australian Jack, but trust me, nobody's *that* Australian."

```
TDSTMP:    121815.0800Z
PRTY:      STANDARD

SNDR:      KOROMO BASE

TRGT:      GHQ

SITREP:    FIREBASE ALPHA AND BRAVO
           RECONSTRUCTION COMPLETE.
           FIREBASE CHARLIE STILL
           BEING CLEARED. FIREBASE
           DELTA LOCATION HAS BEEN
           DETERMINED. SCOUTS ARE
           LOOKING FOR FIREBASE ECHO
           SITE. NO ENEMY CONTACT.

[END TRANSMISSION]
```

Chapter 15

December 18, 2015

Jack was walking down the main aisle toward the part of Business Unit Six where their Learner's Storyboard was set up. On this board the team was vigilantly recording each step of the improvement kata, by the book. The steady hum of the machinery, the sharp ripping of the saws, the deep thrumming of the air makeup units over by the powder-coating line all kept him company as he thought about the upcoming line review. Jack sub-consciously patted his jacket pocket for the third time since he left his office, making sure his Coaching Kata card was still there. Thankfully, it hadn't moved in the last three minutes.

For the last eight weeks Jack had been the key learner leading the Improvement Kata team here in Business Unit Six coached by Tony and Pete Valensky, the supervisor. Pete was learning the Coaching Kata as Jack and the team were learning the Improvement Kata. Jack and the team did experiment after experiment as they struggled to overcome one obstacle after another. Some of their experiments had been failures, which at first made everyone on the team feel frustrated. Tony struck to his line that there were no failures as long as they learned. And he was right. Over time they the failures deepened their understanding of their processes, and the failures led to some successes, moving their performance higher as they worked to attain the coveted 'Next Target Condition.'

In the end, the team Jack was working with didn't meet their first Target Condition in the allotted time. They had given themselves a month and it took them five weeks to get there. They were disappointed a bit, but then they moved to the next Target Condition and found they had the skill to define it more precisely. The percent successful increased and they found they were even energized by the failures which simply meant their hypothesis was not confirmed. Thinking scientifically had its advantages.

During the shift they, of course, had to run production, but Jack was frequently called over to one station after another to quickly capture an idea or two as the operators thought about the next Obstacle that they were addressing. The team would agree on what to try next and the experiment was set up and run and the results were checked against their expectations.

As the team, Jack included, got more experienced with the process, including the routine of Pete, who was under the watchful eye of Tony, asking them the coaching questions and providing corrective feedback, Jack noticed a subtle change in the people. They were talking about things in a different way. Before, if people were asked for ideas, you would hear things like "Here is my idea to solve this problem. I'm confident it will work." It might have been a very solid idea, and it might have yielded an improvement if implemented. However, it might not be addressing something critical to the business and it might simply be transforming waste from one form to another, which Jack found to be a very common outcome. For example, people used to convert motion waste to the waste of waiting, as the redesigned workplace reduced the amount of steps a person needed to take, but that excess capacity was never filled, and now the person had no value-adding work to do and just waited.

Now, people were less willing to jump to conclusions. If you asked them for improvement ideas they would fire back with a question like: 'Which Obstacle are we working on and how does it relate to the Target Condition?" When they tried an idea and it worked they would spontaneously start discussing what they learned from it. A successful outcome by itself was not enough.

These were very specific questions that, in Jack's opinion, sharpened everyone's thinking to the point that what used to be 'squishy' ideas now came out much clearer and sharper. He would hear things from the team like 'Since we're still wrestling with the clamping on the assembly fixture, I have an idea about moving the single action push clamp to the other side of the work piece to better close that gap.' The team would then discuss the idea and agree on an expected outcome. Yes, they decided after looking at the fixture design, if they moved the clamps to a different location they might well close up a critical joint and eliminate the rework that was driving their costs away from their target. Then they got excited about testing their proposition.

This way of thinking and understanding each individual process was new to the organization and it was, Jack thought, an incredibly powerful approach. These new practice routines, as Tony called them, were teaching everyone involved, which at this point went from Charlie through Geoff and Pete, down to the value-adding teams. Everyone involved got to see and experience, firsthand, the power behind disciplined, scientific thinking.

Jack could remember the days when people would just make a 'guestimate' on something and then a group of people would 'try-storm' a bunch of ideas and see if anything improved. Any and all improvements were then celebrated and the teams usually moved on to another 'project.' With the Kata approach, the teams were all turning into scientists and their work areas were their own little, self-contained laboratories, where they could create a hypothesis, design an experiment, run the experiment, and check the results against their hypothesis. They didn't use these terms, of course, but that's exactly what was happening in the Business Units where the Kata were being deployed. It was truly a new and fascinating way to look at process improvement and operational excellence, in Jack's opinion.

In the preceding two months, Jack progressed quickly in his understanding of the Improvement Kata and Tony suggested he try his hand at coaching. For the last week Jack had been performing the role of the Coach for the newly minted Team Leader out in Business Unit Six. They had proposed the Team Leader role before, but now they had a much clearer rationale for the role. They desperately needed leaders of continuous improvement. The supervisors simply did not have the bandwidth to coach dozens of people when they were spending most of their time fire-fighting. At best a good learner leading a Kata project could work with groups of 4-7 people, just the recommended scope of a Team Leader's responsibility. This would also complete the chain of coaching from Charlie all the way through the team, which was one of Charlie's objectives: train excellent coaches throughout the chain that can eventually serve as Second Coach as the deployment continued.

After the Flanders 'takeover' of the company, Jack again pitched the need for the Team Leader position on the shop floor, its having been eliminated earlier in the year as a form of 'cost cutting' prior to the planned IPO. Charlie, having been convinced by Jack that it was critical to success, went to Zack Flanders to talk about adding that level of structure into the operations. Zack was a bit wary, now that he had a huge financial sword hanging over his head, and didn't want to risk defaulting on his new obligations. With further conversations Charlie convinced him that the *only* way they were going to hit the challenges they need to hit, both short term and long term, was to put the Team Leaders in place in the Business Units to begin their own Improvement Kata journeys. Specialized, 'SWAT' teams simply weren't going to be able to help the areas fast enough, nor were their efforts going to be sustainable in the long term.

Fortunately they were getting results and Zack Flanders was becoming a true believer. So the Team Leader positions were revitalized at Amalgamated, and candidates were put forward and a few were finishing up their required training curriculum. Kelli and Thanh were also completing their own assignments leading Improvement Kata teams in Business Unit Eight. Tony had been using Pate Valensky, the Business Unit Six supervisor, to coach both Kelli and Thanh to get him more practice as a coach. This also gave Geoff Mueller more experience with the Coaching Kata as he was working with another Business Unit. As per Charlie's earlier mandate, Business Units Four and Two were still working to re-stabilize their areas after having been the victims of the old Kaizen Blast methods driven by Shiloh. Some fences took a bit more time than others to mend, but they were doing much better now and were interested in starting their own Improvement Kata journey after seeing what the other areas were doing.

"G'day Jack," said Tony from behind the guardrail that separated the walking aisle from the production area of Business Unit Six. Tony had on his ubiquitous gray shop coat, complete with multiple mechanical pencils stuck into pockets on the upper right arm and his Day-Timer held in front of his crossed arms like a shield.

"Morning Tony," said Jack as he made his way through the opening in the guard rail and walked with Tony toward the team's Learner's Storyboard. Jack reached up and patted his pocket again.

"Is it still in there mate, or has she made a break for it?" asked Tony, who noticed Jack's sub-conscious movement.

"What? Oh yes, yes," Jack said smiling, "it's still in there. Is it that obvious?"

"Yeah mate, it is. Just relax, you're doing fine." said Tony with his usual smile. That was high praise from Tony, who seldom doled out praise, choosing instead to reflect on what happened, what went right, what went wrong, and what course corrections were needed. Jack knew it was for his benefit, and he appreciated Tony's professionalism and dedication to making Jack a better coach. The old catchphrase of 'learn by doing' was taking on a whole new meaning for Jack.

"Hi Jack, hey Tony," said Kate Drayton, the newly minted team leader out in the Business Unit. Kate was fairly new to Amalgamated, having less than five years with the company, but she was seen both by her peers as well as Pete, her supervisor, as a person with high potential. When the team put forward her name as a candidate for Team Leader, the agreement was unanimous. Kate finished the Team Leader curriculum with honors in less than a month, which was a new record for Amalgamated. She completed the on-line portion of the training in a week and took the required courses outside of working hours at the local community college, which had agreed to run some of the training programs for Amalgamated. Charlie already had her pegged as someone to keep an eye on for further opportunities.

"G'day Kate," said Tony, "how ya goin' awright?"

"Doing well, Tony, thank you. The team and I have made some good progress that we're eager to show you."

"Excellent," this from Jack, "so let's go and see." They walked over to the Kata storyboard. Jack pulled out his laminated 2-sided Coaching Kata card from his jacket pocket and began reading from it.

"So Kate, tell me what your target condition is here?" began Jack, without looking up from his card. Tony smiled slightly at Jack's stony countenance as he tried to be as 'coachy' as he could.

"Same as yesterday Jack," replied Kate, "We're trying to get our total unit cost down to $14.85 for the product family by improving yield which will require getting our end of line quality to 98% first time through and reduce our customer returns to less than one a month. As a result of the quality improvements we will be able to produce more in the same amount of time. And we want to complete this by the end of the month which will be four weeks of experimenting."

"So, what is the actual condition now?" asked Jack, still looking intently at the card in his hand.

"Well," said Kate, "we're running at $16.50 for the product line, our first time through is at 88%, and we've had two customer returns already this month."

Jack said quietly 'turn card over' and dutifully turned the card over and began reading from the back. "So, Kate, what did you plan as your last step?"

Kate smiled at Jack's dedication to reading the Coaching Kata card exactly as printed. "Our last step was to change around our clamping scheme on the chair backs to reduce some of the variation we were finding."

Still looking down at his card, Jack asked "So, what did you expect would happen?"

"We expected to improve our first time through to 90%, dropping our unit cost down to $16.25," Kate replied.

Tony leaned closer to Jack and quietly said "mate, you don't have to stare holes in the bloody card, take a mo and look at your team leader."

Jack, looked up quickly at Kate, saw her looking at him with arched eyebrows, a grin, and slowly waving 'hello,' and started smiling himself. A little too rigid, he thought to himself. "Sorry Kate, I didn't mean to be so oblivious, I just want to get this right. For my benefit as well as the team's."

"No problem Jack," laughed Kate, "we *appreciate* your stoic adherence to the process. I know that your next question is going to be to ask me what actually happened when we ran the experiment, right?" Jack looked down at his card, smiled and nodded to Kate.

"Anyway," she continued, "we basically got most of what we wanted on that little experiment, but fell short of our expectations due to some variation in both our process as well as the materials coming in to us."

"So," said Jack, "what did you learn from this experiment?"

"We learned," said Kate, "that our expectation to hit a home run with every experiment was unrealistic."

"Good, good," said Jack as he quietly said to himself 'return to question 3' and turned the card back over. He looked up at Kate and then said "What Obstacles do you think are preventing you from reaching the target condition?"

"All of these, pick one," said Kate as she pointed to the Obstacle parking lot on her team's Learner's Storyboard. The list was nine items long and two were already crossed out, showing that they had been overcome in prior experiments.

"Oh, ok," said Jack, "and which one are you and the team addressing now?"

"We're still working on this one," she said pointing to the board, "the assembly process variation obstacle. This will be our fifth experiment coming up. We're two and two on this one. Our first two experiments, you'll recall," Kate was now pointing to the PDCA Cycles Record sheet on her Learner's Storyboard, "ended badly and gave us no improvements, but the next two were successful. It just took us a few tries to really get going."

"What is your next step?" asked Jack patiently reading the questions but looking a bit antsy.

Kate dutifully replied, "Our clamping strategy is inadequate for this complex of a product. Engineering just copied the strategy from the more basic products, but these products need a more robust plan to keep them in place while we do the assembly operations."

"Yes, I remember," said Jack, getting reenergized, "So your next step is going to be to change the clamping strategy. That's smart. Some of those parts will need at least two clamps, and maybe spring-loaded at that, to keep them stable during the assembly process."

Kate thought about that for a second, "Yes, you're probably right Jack."

Jack was about to make another suggestion to Kate when he noticed Tony staring intently at him, trying to get his attention. Jack glanced at Tony long enough to see him, almost imperceptibly, shaking his head 'no.' Jack caught himself, closed his eyes, and took a deep breath before saying, "Kate, forget I said that," now he was looking at his card again, "and tell me what do you expect will happen as a result of your next experiment?."

"Ok Jack," said Kate, still smiling, "we expect to get to our $16.25 unit cost and 90% first time through.

"Excellent, excellent," said Jack, "so how quickly can we go and see what we have learned from taking that step?"

"Hmm," Kate began, "I've already talked to Tim over in fixture repair and he's coming over during our last break to talk to us about what we need done. Plus, he's been doing this for a while and I'm sure he can give us some suggestions." Since we're only hitting Tim up late today with this, he's probably going to want another day to plan for the changes and make the necessary modifications. Given that, I'd say give us until the day after tomorrow and come back and we'll show you how we're doing."

"Excellent, excellent," said Jack, "I'm eager to see how the improvements worked out. See you tomorrow Kate."

"Bye Jack, bye Tony," said Kate with a smile and a wave. Tony gave Kate a brief nod and a 'thumbs up' and walked out of the area with Jack. Jack was carefully putting his Improvement Kata card back into his pocket.

"Harder than it looks, isn't it Jack?" asked Tony.

"Which part?" asked Jack.

"The part," continued Tony, "where you stop giving them ideas and focus on their thinking."

Jack was frowning at his mistake during the report out and shook his head. "Yeah, I blew that one didn't I?"

"Nah mate, no worries, she'll be right. Helps to have a team leader with a sense of humor" said Tony smiling.

"I suppose," said Jack as they continued to walk back up to the office area. "But it's harder than it seems. I've spent my career trying to help people work through problems. Most of the time I'd offer suggestions or nudges because I'd already 'seen this movie' if you know what I mean."

"I do, Jack; I do," said Tony, "but don't forget that your biggest, most important role here is not to offer suggestions, but to ensure that your team is following a good process. That they're thinking through what they're trying to do and what they expect to get. We're trying to get people out of the habit of just long-jumping in a dark room and being happy with whatever they get. We're reinforcing the 'predict – try – reflect' cycle in the teams that we're coaching. If you ever want to build a world-class Kaizen culture, this is the only way mate, trust me. This is the way we did it at Toyota. And it worked, and maybe would have worked even better if we had all the details of the Kata worked out."

"Of course I trust you, Tony," said Jack, "and I understand what we're trying to do. Sometimes I slip up like I did back there. I guess I haven't yet developed coaching skills as a habit yet, eh?"

"We'll get there Jack, don't worry, we'll get there. You're actually moving at light speed compared to the ideal pace for your brain developing those embedded habits with thick insulation."

"Yeah, I know. I guess I'm a little impatient because I fear if we don't get results fast enough the plug could be pulled. So, how is the rest of my team doing? I've got quite a diverse bunch that I'm working with."

"Kelli," Tony began, "is taking to this like a Koala to a gum tree. Young Thanh is doing ok, but I'm working with him a bit on his approach. He's a bit quiet with his team, but he's getting better.

When we start practicing the Coaching Kata with him in the other Business Unit, I'll be able to address it directly. He's got to learn to give critical feedback. No worries, he'll get there. Your mate Dean, the bloke from Shiloh who somehow survived the reorg, now he's a real project."

"Tell me about it," said Jack in agreement. While Dean had reluctantly left behind the old Kaizen Blast methodology, a lifetime of bad habits took a bit of time to overcome.

"He's bloody smart," continued Tony, "but he's so quick to jump in and cut people off. Seems for him it's a game of one one-upmanship. I'm working with him to dial it back a bit. He'll be kickin' goals before too long mate. Once we get him started on the Coaching Kata, we'll know if he can be salvaged."

"How about Charlie and his leadership team?" asked Jack.

"That man scares me silly Jack, let me tell you. I haven't ever met a larger human being in my life," said Tony smiling.

"Agreed," said Jack.

"But," continued Tony, "he's doing great. He sees the benefit of the approach and he's driving his team pretty hard to make sure they follow the process to the letter. It's obvious they all respect him, 'cause they're working pretty hard to make sure they don't let him down."

"Yeah," agreed Jack, "the teams will break their backs for Charlie, because they know he'll do the same for them. The man inspires loyalty."

"Too right," said Tony, "and Pete Valensky and Geoff Mueller have both been doing well, both with the Improvement Kata as well as the Coaching Kata. Having Pete pull triple duty coaching three Business Units was rough on him, but we needed to have the chains of coaching intact. It needed to be from Charlie to Geoff to Pete. Geoff also got more chances to practice the Coaching Kata with Pete watching the three areas. That was the only way to get Kelli, Thanh, and Dean involved learning the Improvement Kata. After two months of learn-by-doing, I'm pretty happy with the progress of everybody, at all levels of the organization."

"So how long before we expand?" asked Jack. "I understand this is a starter kata in the novice stage where we mostly copy exactly the pattern. How long will it be before we move beyond the novice stage to something more intermediate where we can begin to improvise on the approach? Are we getting close?"

Tony laughed. "Jack Hartmann, you need to let this work itself out. You'll know when you get there." Tony stopped for a second and looked down, deep in thought. "Nah, forget that mate, you won't know when you get there, you'll just realize one day that you're there. Nobody shoots off any party poppers or anything. You just keep evolving as you get better. At Toyota anyone with less than five years of deep practice was a novice, pure and simple. This isn't something where you can do some kind of fancy audit and the scores will tell you that somehow 'you've arrived at the intermediate skill phase'."

"Great." said Jack, not convinced.

"C'mon," said Tony, "let me buy you a coffee and we'll head back to the office and see if Kelli has killed Dean yet."

"That's not funny Tony," said Jack, "the last thing she needs is encouragement."

Tony just grinned, slapped Jack on the back and the two of them headed down the main aisle toward the cafeteria.

```
TDSTMP:    021516.1310Z
PRTY:      STANDARD

SNDR:      KOROMO BASE

TRGT:      GHQ

SITREP:    PATROLS REPORT LIGHT ENEMY
           CONTACT. NO CASUALTIES
           SUSTAINED. DIFFICULTIES
           CLEARING PARTS OF FIREBASE
           CHARLIE. SUPPLY OF MATERIAL
           AND AMMO TO FIREBASE DELTA
           COMMENCED. FIREBASE ECHO
           UNDER CONSTRUCTION.

[END TRANSMISSION]
```

Chapter 16

February 15, 2016

Jack, holding his steaming, antique mug of coffee, walked carefully through the production offices and was heading to Charlie's conference room. He greeted the production engineering team that was present as he made his way past the desks, file cabinets, and print tables, the latter being a throwback to a previous age. Charlie liked to review engineering's proposal layouts and documents on the table, so it remained a fixture in the production offices. Jack walked past Taylor Smith's desk, giving her a smile and a nod as he tried not to spill any of his steaming coffee as he walked. Taylor waved him into the conference room with a cheery "Hello Jack, how's it going this morning?"

"Good Taylor, thank you." he said by way of reply. Jack made his way into Charlie's conference room where he saw Thanh and Kelli sitting at the conference room table. He walked to the nearest open chair, carefully put down his coffee mug, pulled out the chair, and sat down. Kelli had her laptop open and was polishing off a few emails before the meeting got underway.

"I cannot *believe* that mug is still alive," said Kelli with a smile and a shake of the head. "You know, boss-man, you cost me twenty bucks in the pool."

The 'pool,' was the wager when Jack's ancient coffee mug would finally break. Which, by looking at all of the chips and cracks on the thing, could be any day now. Of course, that's what Kelli thought four months ago when she picked Christmas as her cutoff date.

"Sorry Kelli," said Jack as he smiled and carefully took a sip of the over-full mug of coffee. "What can I say; they don't build 'em like this anymore." Jack patted the side of the mug and carefully set it back down on the desk.

"That's probably lead paint on the side you know," said Kelli, "since that thing was probably cast back in the bronze age."

Jack smiled at Kelli's barb, amazed himself that his prized mug was still in one piece. It was a well-known secret that the pool had been going on since the first week Jack had found the artifact upstairs in the abandoned conference room's storage closet. The one with the rats.

Next to walk into the conference room was Dean, who exchanged 'hellos' with everyone before taking his seat next to Thanh. Jack was happy to see that Thanh and Dean had buried the hatchet, as it were, and were getting along very well. It was, Jack thought, a good arrangement in that Thanh and Dean were basically complementary personalities. Where Dean was brash and forward, Thanh was more introspective and thoughtful. It didn't take long for them to figure out that they were pretty evenly matched, intellectually, so their quiet competition was to see who could be the best coach to their respective team. Dean still has his quick wit and sharp tongue, but he had toned it down enough to fit comfortably within the realm of accepted behavior. Plus, Jack thought, Kelli still was reserving the right to run him through the sawmill if things ever got out of hand again.

Next, Geoff Mueller and Pete Valensky walked through the door with Kate Drayton and they took empty seats around the conference table after exchanging morning pleasantries with the group. Jack noticed that amongst Geoff's pile of papers he had fresh copies of the skills matrices that were developed months ago with the dogged determination of Carrie Anderson and her team of Human Resources associates.

Carrie had recently returned to the Amalgamated site after a brief stint over at the Shiloh facility. She and her team had moved into the space vacated by Steve Bucholtz after the private equity firm left the picture. Carrie had asked Charlie about clearing the office space to make room for her and three of her associates, and Charlie readily agreed to convert the space.

What Charlie didn't count on was having to remove the entire door frame and part of the hallway to get the massive desk set and bookcases out. It took two carpenters and four millwrights the better part of a day removing enough structure to get the items out into the hallway and the next day to get them wrapped and strapped, ready for transport. Charlie's next big problem was that he had no idea where to ship them. Nobody at either facility had an interest and Charlie didn't want to just chop them up for kindling, so he was at a bit of an impasse. This problem was solved when Kate Drayton mentioned that the community college where she had been taking her courses for her Team Leader curriculum would probably love to have the furniture. The place was, she told Charlie, quite Spartan in its décor and those pieces would make it look much more academic. Charlie agreed and made the appropriate phone calls and it all worked out.

With Carrie back on board, the focus on people development at the Amalgamated site was re-energized, with her and her team leading the charge to improve and expand their focus on improving their workforce's skills and abilities. It turned out the method she was using for developing skills, derived from the World War II *Training Within Industry* program was really another form of Kata. Standard Work was broken down to job instructions with key points which were drilled repetitively until they became habits for the learner. Their efforts were applauded by all involved and Jack surmised that Geoff and Pete had just come from a meeting with the HR people about his team's development progress.

The last two to join the group were Tony and Charlie, with Tony greeting the group with his usual 'G-day team,' and Charlie with his usual gruff 'ladies and gents' as he set down his thirty two ounce cup of steaming coffee and sat down at the table.

"Thank you all for coming," Charlie began, "I called this meeting on Tony's advice so we can talk a bit about what we've been doing for the last three months or so. He called it a 'quarterly reflection' so that's what we're going to start calling them. He tried to get me to call them a Hans Solo something or other, but I think *reflection* will do just fine." Kelli laughed out loud and quickly covered her mouth at Charlie's attempt at 'hansei,' the Japanese word for reflection. This got her a stern look from Charlie as he was putting on his reading glasses. She gave him a sheepish grin and took a quick sip of her coffee-based drink.

"Anyway," Charlie went on, still holding his stare on Kelli, "there's some things we need to cover. The first is around the coaching process and personnel development and the second is on expansion. So, let's start with the coaching first."

Everyone looked at Tony, thinking that he was going to be leading the discussion around the topic since he was, everybody knew, the expert in the room. When Charlie kept talking, the attendees briefly exchanged surprised looks.

"What we've been doing for the last five months or so," Charlie said, "is developing a true chain of coaching." Charlie seemed to look down the table at Tony for approval, who gave him the briefest of nods and a slight smile. "Kate, as Team Leader you've been coaching your team on the Improvement Kata for the last two months. So you've gotten some great experience at being a Coach."

"True," replied Kate, "this has been a little tougher than I thought, but I think I'm getting the hang of what it takes to be a coach rather than just the next level of supervision."

Geoff leaned in and asked, "So what have been your biggest challenges Kate?"

"Hey," from Dean, "shouldn't we talk a bit about all the great things she's done with her team? I mean come on; they've knocked out, what, three obstacles in the last two weeks?"

"Who are you and what have you done with Dean?" asked Kelli with a wide-eyed grin. Thanh laughed and even Jack had to smile. Dean had come a long way from their first caustic meeting those many months ago.

"Yeah, yeah," Dean shot back, "can the sarcasm kid, I didn't mean to cut you off Geoff."

"No sweat Dean," said Geoff, "Maybe you're—"

"No, it's fine," said Kate, "Really, I—"

"Problems are good," said Tony. The group fell silent and looked down to the end of the table where Tony was looking down and flipping the pages of his ever-present day timer. He flipped one more page and then looked up at the group, who were waiting to see what was going to come next.

"Problems are a good thing to have. It means you can get better by solving them. At this point learning is more important than knocking off obstacles. That's something you need to program up here," he said, touching his temple, "and something you need to believe in here," he finished while tapping his heart.

The group let that sink in a little bit and kept looking at Tony, waiting to see if he was going to add any clarification to that point.

"Don't forget gang," he went on, "that your job, as Kate said earlier, is to first learn through the Improvement Kata how to lead improvement, and then learn how to be a good *coach*, not a good boss or manager. Those are different things entirely. The whole reason you are practicing the Kata is to learn to improve yourself. If Kate runs into some problems, she needs to be able to work with her coach. Her coach should be able to help her make any course corrections and give her critical feedback to help keep her on her path of self-development."

"I thought we were trying to ditch the whole 'critical' thing," said Dean.

"Critical feedback," continued Tony, "is part of the 'Respect for People' pillar in the Toyota Way. It's not *being* critical of someone, it's not fault-finding, but rather honest feedback on what the coach sees. We're trying to be hard on the problem, team, not hard on the person. I know you've all got some history here with the recent merger, but you need to get back to the way you used to operate, from what Charlie has been telling me." Tony looked at Charlie with raised eyebrows searching for corroboration.

"True," said Charlie, "even though we didn't have the Improvement Kata as our foundation stone, we always treated each other with respect, even when we didn't agree. It was during last year's merger and IPO attempt that we lost our way, so to speak. It shouldn't be too hard to stamp out that little problem."

"Sounds great to me," said Tony, "because each of you is going to be playing both roles in the chain of coaching. You're going to be a coach and you're going to be learners *being* coached as you work on your own Challenges. So why don't we kick it back down to Kate and let her finish her thoughts on the problems she's having as a coach, shall we?" Tony smiled and looked from face to face. When nobody spoke up, he pointed down the table to Kate, smiled, and made a 'come on' gesture with his hand.

"Well," she began, "I think the toughest challenge for me, initially, was sticking to the process without deviation. I mean, I know I had the laminated card with the questions on it and all, but sometimes I'd find myself skipping ahead because I thought I knew everything there was to know about an experiment, or I'd just make assumptions and keep plowing ahead. My focus was more on the results rather than the process."

Pete was nodding at what Kate was saying, as he was performing the role of her coach during this process. "I know," he said, "that the process can seem cumbersome, especially when you keep asking the same questions repeatedly. For me, the hardest part has been to slow down and follow the process instead of offering answers and direction. Kate, to her credit, has been patient and understands that the Coaching Kata isn't something you just wake up knowing how to do. So, I keep focusing on learning to be a better coach and not some kind of efficiency guru."

"I get that too, Pete," said Kate, "when you know so much about the process or area or product, it's easy to jump to conclusions and short-circuit the whole thing, which just short-circuits the entire learning process for the team."

"Yeah," this from Dean, "I have really been workin' on that too Kate. So I feel your pain. I gotta stop myself from jumpin' in and just tellin' the teams what to do instead of listening and makin' sure they're followin' the process like they're s'posed to."

"That's why," said Tony, smiling, "you all have those handy dandy cards in your pockets. Too keep you on track. And don't be too hard on yourselves, because I've seen worse gang, a *lot* worse. You just need to keep in mind that you're creating the habit of thinking scientifically, and not just jumping to the first conclusion that comes to mind."

"I'm guilty too," said Charlie, looking up and down the table, "but I know that sticking to the script is going to be the way we get there, and I know you all do too. So we just need to keep trying and make sure we don't let anybody struggle or go off the rails with the process. Like Tony said, we're creating habits by practicing every day and getting some good coaching. We'll get there team, I have faith in each and every one of you. Even you, short round." Charlie was looking over his reading glasses at Kelli, who made a face and took another noisy sip of her coffee-type drink. This got a hoot from Dean, who quickly quieted down when he got a withering stare from Kelli, remembering that he was still on 'double secret probation,' whatever that was.

"I have faith," said Tony, "that you mob are going to be just fine as long as you stick to the program. It's structured for a reason. You don't just wake up one morning and 'Bob's your uncle!' you've got a whole new skill set. Be patient."

Charlie looked with an arched eyebrow down to Kelli for a quick translation and she silently mouthed the word 'voila' to Charlie, who smiled and nodded once in understanding. Some of Tony's more colorful slang still eluded Charlie, but he was picking up speed in translating his own coach's approach.

"I think we're ok there Tony," said Jack, "especially since this chain of coaching idea that we're following pretty much guarantees that we're all going to be supporting one another throughout the process."

"Agreed Jack," said Charlie, "we might be learning at different speeds because we're working on and coaching different problems in the company, but I haven't seen any real behaviors that worry me. I spend a fair amount of time talking with Zack about how it's going, especially since he's now trying to land new product lines that'll keep both sites busy for the next few years."

"Awesome!" said Kelli, "that's great news. But won't that mess up what we're doing now?" Kelli looked down the table at Tony, whose reply was a grin as he looked around the table to see who was going to answer her.

"Not really Kelli," said Kate, "I guess it will in the short run, especially if it involves some new equipment and processes, but doesn't that mean we just work on a new Challenge?"

"True," agreed Kelli, "it shouldn't matter *what* problems you're working on, it's the *how* you're working that's important. Your honor, I withdraw the question," said Kelli looking at Charlie, who was smiling and nodding.

"Agreed again," said Charlie, "but that brings us to the second reason we're talking here today, and that is the speed with which we're deploying the Kata methodologies. The way I see it, we're going as fast as we can, given that the total number of coaches were have is exactly, let's see," he made a show of pointing at and counting everyone in the room, "eight, plus our head coach, Tony. And in reality the eight are really coaches in training who are barely qualified to be good learners."

"Well done Jolly Green," said Kelli with a smile, "good thing we didn't have more than ten."

"Watch it short round," said Charlie as he looked over his reading glasses down the table at Kelli, "you're still under investigation for the infamous 'Cooks family photo' scandal." Jack smiled at the memory of that particular prank. He still couldn't figure out how she managed to pull it off.

"The bigger problem," continued Charlie, "is that we're going to be, potentially, introducing a lot more product into both facilities and we need to be sharp when we do it. The financials won't support a sloppy or delayed launch on any of the lines. Zack Flanders is really putting us on the spot here, but after the last five months, I'm sure we can rise to the challenge. I've been talking to Tony here," Charlie gestured down the table to Tony, "and we're ready to begin our expansion over at Shiloh." This pronouncement shocked the group, as even though they'd been working on their own deployment for about six months, including the initial training, they knew they needed far more experience. Charlie let his pronouncement sink in for a few moments before continuing.

"So what we're going to do, starting next month is have Dean and Thanh work at Shiloh with their Business Unit 3. They're working right now on getting their two business unit leaders, day and night shift, through the curriculum.

"I know that area," said Dean, "they're pretty sharp. Some of this is going to be pretty scary stuff to the night shift business unit leader and the supervisor though Charlie, I'd bet my next paycheck on it."

Charlie looked at Dean, considering his remark, and then smiled. "Dean," said Charlie, "I wouldn't take your money on such an easy bet."

Dean thought for a minute, staring at the table in front of him and drumming his fingers until he finally looked up, snapped his fingers, and said "you're bringing them here too, aren't you?"

Charlie nodded at Dean, happy his newest team member quickly discerned his moves and motives. "You're going to bring them here to shadow Geoff and Pete. Makes sense. Then Thanh and I will work with them at Shiloh and they'll have a peer over here to talk to as well. Nice. Very nice."

"I'm glad you approve, Mr. Berzani," Charlie said, "I don't want anybody, at either site, going around either half-cocked or half-trained. We need to do this right and we'll roll into as many Business Units into this as we have coaches trained up. Having gone through this for the last six or so months with Tony looking over my shoulder, I get it that this isn't a two week program." Tony was nodding in agreement at the end of the table and stood up and picked up his Day Timer.

"Well gang," Tony began, "I'm pretty happy with where we're at so far, and I'll be here for the next ten weeks working with you on the internal and external expansion. But, that'll bring my full time support here to an end." A frown creased Kelli's face as she digested the news. While he wasn't yet the new Mr. O'Malley, she hadn't given up hope. The others in the room began to start grumbling amongst themselves until Charlie broke in.

"Team, we're not losing Tony," he said, "we're just not going to have him here full time. The man has other commitments. We were lucky that Zack was able to get him here for as long as he did."

"Thanks Charlie," said Tony, "it's not that you're done gang, far from it. And you know it. The problem is I can't really be effective as a coach on a part-time basis. This is something that you need to do every day. Practice every day. This isn't something you can just phone in. I can stop by every month or so and give you some outsiders' feedback, but the hard yards of creating and developing coaches will fall squarely on your shoulders."

"So Tony," said Dean, "you're saying that bringing in consultants for Kaizen Blasts, like we used to do, isn't effective?"

"You tell me," said Tony in response. Dean thought for a minute, rubbed his chin, and nodded at Tony.

"Tony," asked Kelli, "do other consultants know that you tell companies this?"

Tony quickly looked behind him to the left and right and held up a finger to his lips. "Don't tell anyone or me goose is cooked." This got a laugh from the room.

"Ok team," said Charlie, "if there isn't anything else, Geoff, why don't you stick around and let's talk about some of these volume projections. I've asked Tom Donaldson from engineering to stop by. He'll be here in," Charlie looked at his watch, "about fifteen minutes."

Kate looked down at her phone to respond to the texts that had come in during the meeting and Pete got up to leave. Kelli opened up her laptop and waited for the screen to blink to life to check her e-mails. She was rewarded a second later with multiple 'pings' letting her know that her inbox was filling up. Jack got up, grabbed his battered mug, and began to walk to the door.

"Oh my God! No way!" Kelli shouted at her computer, her eyes wide and a look of astonishment washed across her face.

The group froze and immediately all conversation stopped as head turned toward Kelli. Jack almost dropped his mug as he hurried around the table to see what Kelli was looking at, now with both hands covering her mouth and her eyes bugged out. Thanh, Kate, and Dean hurried around the table as Geoff looked at Charlie, looking for some insight. He just shrugged and got up to see what had gotten Kelli so upset. Pete came around the table and joined the group, all straining to see Kelli's laptop screen.

"Is that—" began Dean.

"It is!" said Thanh. "That's amazing!" Kelli still had both hands over her mouth, eyes wide, now shaking her head.

"Hey, it's Gary," said Kate, looking over Kelli's left shoulder at her screen, "wow, it sure is beautiful there. Is that Italy? That's a fancy looking boat. And wow, look at the *size* of that thing."

"It's Lake Como," said Kelli, hands still over her mouth. Jack had remembered that Thanh and Kelli had showed Gary how to set up an Instagram account, and he had obviously taken the time to upload some photos.

"What?" said Kate, "how do you know?"

"Because," said Kelli as she removed her hands from her mouth and pointed at the screen, "that is GEORGE.....CLOONEY!!!"

"What?" said Kate, as she squinted at the screen, and then she gasped as she recognized the actor smiling back at the camera, deeply tanned, an arm draped around Gary Peterson's shoulders.

Everyone took turns crowding around Kelli's laptop to look at the photo and verify for themselves that their friend had, somehow, shared a meal with the Hollywood actor. There was laughter and good feelings all around as the meeting finally broke up, the various members left, and Charlie and Geoff returned to their discussions around future volume projections.

"See you this arvo Jack," said Tony as he turned left outside of the production offices and walked down the aisle.

"Ok Tony, see you then," replied Jack as he turned right and headed for the staircase that led up to the second floor's east conference room where he liked to quietly think.

He opened the heavy, fireproof, metal door and began climbing the stairs, his steel shanked boots ringing off the metal stairs as he ascended. The sounds of the factory slowly fading as the door swung closed. George Clooney. Wow. Good for you, Gary, good for you…

```
TDSTMP:      041516.0930Z
PRTY:        STANDARD

SNDR:        KOROMO BASE

TRGT:        GHQ

SITREP:      FIREBASE CHARLIE REPORTS
             SITE CLEARED. RE-SUPPLY OF
             FIREBASE DELTA COMPLETE.
             PATROLS REPORT INCREASING
             ENEMY CONTACT. ENEMY TROOPS
             MASSING BEYOND THRESHOLD.
             OFFENSIVE APPEARS TO BE
             FORMING TO THE NORTHEAST.

[END TRANSMISSION]
```

Chapter 17

April 15, 2016

Charlie's conference room was now the de-facto debriefing room for the coaches as they continued to deploy the Improvement Kata and Coaching Kata. It was big enough, but not over-large for the group, keeping a feeling of closeness amongst the participants, which is what Charlie wanted.

Taylor Smith was setting up a coffee urn in the corner and tearing the thin plastic sleeve off of a stack of paper coffee cups emblazoned with the Amalgamated logo. These were a gift from a local vendor looking to land a kitchen supply contract with the company. Taylor was only too happy to accept them and immediately put them to use. She stacked the cups next to the urn and double-checked that the sugar, sweeteners, and creamer, both liquid and powder, were adequate and then put a manila folder in front of the chair that Charlie usually occupied. Satisfied with the conference room's setup, Taylor walked out of the conference room and headed into the production supervisor's area to attend an informal, weekly meeting on morale and people development.

Jack and Kelli were the first to arrive, Kelli with her giant coffee-based drink and Jack carrying his battered coffee mug. Taylor had told the team that coffee would be provided, so Jack dutifully headed to the urn to get himself a fresh cup. Kate and Pete followed soon after and everyone took a seat around Charlie's table and chatted about current happenings out on the floor. Thanh came in next with a steaming cup of his favorite chai tea, smiled and nodded to the assembled group, and took a seat around the table. A minute later Dean walked in with the Shiloh people, Susan Thompson, the Business Unit Manager, and Mina Shirin, the area supervisor. They both had the forest green shop coats worn by Shiloh people. They greeted everyone present, headed for the coffee urn, and each filled up steaming cups of coffee. Mina looked at the logo on the paper cup, then at Susan, smiled, and took a sip. Next to arrive was Tony, who walked in and gave his standard 'g'day troops' to the assembled group and took a seat. Charlie was the last to arrive and greeted the assembled group before taking his seat at the table. He briefly opened the folder in front of him, scanned the top sheet in the pile, smiled briefly, and closed the folder.

"Ok team," Charlie began, "let's get going. I don't think this will take the full half hour, but let's see." The assembled group nodded and all heads turned to Kate Drayton, the team leader.

"My turn this week, eh?" said Kate, "ok, my team is responding a lot better with the Improvement Kata. We've been working on our obstacles and doing a good job of running our experiments. It took a few times through the process to convince my team that we really need to buckle down and think a little harder about what we're trying to do. As you all know, this isn't exactly something that comes naturally. We've really got to focus."

"Excellent Kate," said Tony, "this doesn't need to be natural, because for most folks it isn't, but it does need to be a habit. That's what we're working for here, to create the *habit* of thinking in a scientific way. To be able to set a challenge, assess where you are, identify the obstacles, and then start hammering away at them, one at a time. I think you and your team are coming along very well Kate."

"Thank you Tony," beamed Kate, "I'll pass that along to the team."

"All of you," continued Tony, "are working hard at developing these skills into a habit. I know it can be frustrating at times, and feel like you're not going far enough fast enough, but trust me folks, in the long run you'll be miles ahead."

"So let me ask you Tony," this from Charlie, "it's been what, now, almost seven months since we met you over at Tri-Star for our initial three day training? And since then we've been focusing on developing every link in our chain of coaching, as you called it. You've got Kate coaching her team, Pete coaching Kate, Geoff coaching Pete, me coaching Geoff, and Jack's CI team are working on their own chains training up the respective people in the business units."

"Sounds about right Charlie," agreed Tony.

"So," continued Charlie, "are we going fast enough? Are we going too fast? Your feedback is that we're on track, but when you leave, how do we know if we're still on track or if we're headed for problems?"

"No worries Charlie," answered Tony with his usual sardonic grin, "she'll be right." Charlie understood this particular phrase to mean that he was worrying too much. "We've been working on the Improvement Kata and Coaching Kata enough that I have complete confidence that you understand the process of both improvement as well as coaching. You mob are somewhere around the 'Advanced Beginner' stage heading toward 'Competent.'"

"Competent, gee," this from Kelli, "don't worry Tony, our heads won't get too big if you compliment us a little." Kelli smiled and winked at Tony as she took a sip of her large caffeine and sugar-laden concoction.

"I just did," said Tony in response, "after six bloody months to make it beyond 'Novice' is quite an accomplishment." Tony let that sink in for a few seconds before he added "Good job everyone. Well done," and gave each member of the group an exaggerated thumbs up sign. This got a chuckle from Charlie and a few more of the group.

"Ok Tony, Ok," said Charlie, "I know we 'yanks,' as you call us, seem to need constant positive reinforcement, so we'll all take that high praise with a heart-felt thank you."

"Everybody gets a trophy!" exclaimed Tony. Susan and Mina exchanged looks as they just shook their heads. Tony saw the exchange and took the opportunity to address the newest additions to the team.

"Okay Mina, Susan, you've been here at the Amalgamated site now for just over a month and you've been shadowing Pete and Geoff to learn the kata. We've all been talking weekly as a larger group, so give us a summary of your first month's exposure to the Improvement Kata and Coaching Kata."

"Well," Mina began, "I have to say Tony that this is unlike anything we've done over at Shiloh. We've historically been rewarded for delivery regardless of means or process. In that kind of environment, this comes across as a bit of a foreign language."

"Absolutely," added Susan, "Mina's right. Every level of the organization is focused on hitting their numbers, be they quarterly, monthly, or weekly and we build our routines around that. If you deliver the most the fastest, you got promoted. We've got a lot of habits already that do *not* support the adoption of the methodologies that we've been learning here. These are deep habits, too. Most of the higher-seniority people, well, like Mina and me, are really going to have to work to break them." The assembled group listened and nodded, understanding the dedication and focus it takes to truly develop a new habit while letting the old, bad habits die off.

"It's been great here at Amalgamated," said Mina, "working with Pete and Kate learning these routines and I think that they'll be accepted, eventually, at Shiloh." Dean thought about this for a few seconds and raised his hand to get Mina's attention down at the other end of the conference table.

"Wow, really?" quipped Kelly.

"Can it, O'Malley, 'specially since I found out that Charlie don't want nobody getting run through no sawmill." Kelli gave Dean a hard squint followed by a wink.

"Anyways," continued Dean, " Mina, Susan, since we all come from the same system, I wanna hear from you, honestly, how you think we're gonna do when the four of us, Thanh included, go back to Shiloh and start up the first chain of coaching. I'm a bit worried that the culture will totally reject this."

Mina stared at the table as she gathered her thoughts. She looked up, took a deep breath, and answered Dean and the rest of the group. "It's true that our culture is a little bit more 'mechanistic' that the one you've all been building here. And it's also true that the Shiloh site hasn't valued people development to the degree that we've found here, but overall I think that the teams on the floor will respond well to this. I think you've found here that there are a lot of really good ideas coming from very experienced people with deep, functional knowledge of their processes. The Improvement Kata and Coaching Kata help focus their thinking, as well as slow it down, so that people are thinking deeply on an issue and not just shotgun-blasting a huge list of ideas." Susan was nodding, as were Thanh and Dean.

"That's the idea Mina," said Tony, "once we can get the challenge, or direction set, we're able to focus the teams on running their own experiments to improve their process and deepen their own understanding of the process. I haven't found a culture yet where this hasn't resonated. The problem, usually, and no offense to the team here, is that the leadership isn't bought in to the process. They think that this is something they can just delegate, instead of performing their true role, which is to provide strong leadership from the front of the line, so to speak."

"That's still an issue," said Susan, "because Mina and I only represent the middle of the leadership structure over at Shiloh. We don't have the role of team leader and I report in to Charlie's counterpart over at Shiloh, who hasn't had any exposure to this new methodology. He's also one of Shiloh's most senior leaders. I have my doubts about how well we'll be able to deploy these kata. I don't mean to sound down, or cynical, but it's been successful here because Charlie's been such a strong supporter."

"Then you should be fine, Miss Thompson," said Zachary Flanders as he walked into the conference room followed closely by the plant controller, Lyle Whitman. Upon seeing the entry of Messrs. Flanders and Whitman, both Susan and Mina shot to their feet, followed closely by Thanh and Dean. Charlie at first had a quizzical look on his face until he realized that the Shiloh culture demanded that people stand when more senior people enter the conference room. He smiled and looked at the two late-comers with arched eyebrows as if to say 'now what?'

Zack Flanders laughed and said "please sit down you four, but thank you for the honorific." The four exchanged glances, smiled themselves, and regained their seats. "I guess old habits *do* die hard, eh Charlie?"

"I suppose so," agreed Charlie.

"What do you mean, sir, that 'we'll be fine'" asked Mina.

"What I mean is," said Zack, "well, let me back up a bit and have Lyle share with the group what Charlie just found out in my office this morning." Lyle stepped forward and opened a manila folder, a duplicate of the one that sat in front of Charlie on the conference room table.

"Morning all," began Lyle as he looked down at the paper in his hand, "as of September of this year, we will be adding four new, high-volume product lines to Amalgamated and two similar lines will be launching over at Shiloh." The assembled team broke into applause, punctuated by a whistle from Kelli. Thanh and Dean exchanged a high five and Jack's grin went from ear to ear. Kate gave a mock shocked look and clapped her hands to her cheeks. Lyle let the din subside before continuing.

"I agree," said Lyle, "that is this great news. In addition to the high-volume business, we've also greatly expanded our sales for our lower volume product, which will require us to expand our production capacity to afternoon shift and in some cases, a night shift." Lyle let the team absorb the implications of this new information before nodding over to Zack Flanders, who was beaming at the assembled team.

"This will require," added Zack, "a change in leadership structure to manage the increase in our sales channels. This morning Shiloh's operations manager, Oliver Lynch, has announced his retirement after forty one years of service. His retirement will be effective as of June the fifteenth." This got looks of astonishment from the team and a low whistle from Dean. Mina and Susan now understood what Zack's initial comment now meant. With the retirement of Lynch, the chain of coaching would be easier to maintain with someone who would believe in what they were trying to achieve with the Improvement Kata and Coaching Kata.

"This means," continued Zack, "that we will have two gaps in the structure. Mr. Lynch's retirement will open up the Operations Manager position over at Shiloh and we'll also need to find a new Operations Manager here at the Amalgamated site." This last comment got confused looks from the team.

"What happens to Jolly Green?" asked Kelli, mild concern creeping into her voice.

"Mr. Cooks, or 'Jolly Green,' as you call him Miss O'Malley," continued Zack, "will be quite busy in the new role of Vice President of Operations for the corporation." Zack smiled at Charlie, who couldn't help but smile himself as he regarded the stunned faces around the table. Another round of cheers, applause, and whistles ensued to honor the man they all looked up to. Finally, the general thought was, he was being rewarded for his lifetime of service. The applause died down finally, giving Geoff an opportunity to ask a question. Zack saw his raised hand and beckoned him to ask his question.

"This is great and all," began Geoff hesitantly, "and I'm completely thrilled that Charlie's going to be taking on this new role, which he deserves more than anyone, by the way, but I'm thinking about how this is going to affect what we've been doing for the last six or seven months. Isn't this going to open up a big hole in our chain of coaching?"

"Fair point," conceded Zack, "but have no fear Mr. Mueller, we've been working on this for a few months now, and I think that with Mr. McAllister's input," Zack nodded in Tony's direction, "we've been able to chart a very solid succession plan that will ensure that we will lose no ground in our efforts and will only slow our pace enough to skill up the people that will be required to fill any vacancies in the organization. It has always been my intention, and my father's as well, to grow this organization by promoting from within. We spent a lifetime building this company and this culture, so why would we risk disrupting the great work being done here by 'importing,' if you will, a different set of values? It doesn't make any sense to me at all. Does it to you?" Zack surveyed the faces in the room and received shakes of the head from all present. "I didn't think so. So, we'll continue our work with these kata that we've been learning and grow the organization as we need to in order to meet our new challenges. Challenges, I must add, which I am very grateful to have in front of us. I'll leave you now, to continue your meeting, but I want to give you all a very strong 'well done and thank you.' Please pass that along to your team as well, Miss Drayton, if you will."

"Of course," Kate replied.

"Thank you," Zack concluded, "and have a good week. We'll be communicating all of this shortly, including the personnel moves required to support the new structure."

With that, Zack Flanders and Lyle Whitman walked out of the conference room leaving Charlie and the rest of the team to sit silently for a few moments and soak in all of the news. Smiles were exchanged amongst the group and finally Kelli broke the silence.

"Wow, Jolly Green," she began, "I guess we'll all have to be super duper nice to you now, huh?"

Charlie just smiled, shook his head, and took off his reading glasses as he looked around the conference room table.

"Ok short round," Charlie said, "fair enough. I'm proud of the work you've done. All of you. We've been able to not only survive last year's attempted public offering, but we've also been able to strike a new path, with Tony's help, in making us all better thinkers and problem solvers. Without that, I doubt Zack and Lyle would have been as optimistic about us growing around thirty or forty percent in the next six months to a year. For that, Tony, we all owe you a big debt of gratitude."

"No worries Charlie," said Tony with a slight grin, "just don't forget to pay me invoice." This got a snort from Kelli and laughter from the rest of the group.

"But look," Tony continued, "here's the deal. You mob have been working hard on the Improvement Kata and Coaching Kata for over six months and have really been kicking goals, in my humble opinion. You're now expanding over to the Shiloh facility," Tony waved down the table to Susan and Mina, "and the organization is now growing. All of these things are good. I think you all recognize that this isn't something that that you just 'implement' over a weekend, so I'm not worried that you'll lose the plot during the expansion. My only caution is that you don't rush through the development of new people. Take the time to train them right. You know what it takes because you've done it yourselves. As you know I was planning on dialing back my support, but with the new growth coming, Zack has convinced me that I need to stay here longer full time. I told him that I can't do that, but the man in persuasive. So, I'll be around for a few more months working to bring your new people up to speed and I'll be working with your HR group on the overall selection and training process at both sites."

"Speaking of the expansion," said Jack, "Charlie, how is that going to be handled? There's going to be a fair amount of new faces around here and a ton of training is going to have to take place."

"Right you are Mr. Hartmann," answered Charlie, "and to answer your first question, we'll be doing a 'friends and family' outreach first. Any current or former employee can put forward a name or names of people they'd like to start the application process. Always best to have a word of mouth recommendation, right?" This got smiles and nods from the group. "And after that, if we're still short of people, we'll open it up to general hiring. And you're right, we're going to be re-vamping both our hiring process as well as our on-boarding and training processes to deal with this. Carrie Anderson in HR has been locked in a room with her team for the last two weeks laying out what the expansion model will look like so we don't let anybody through the process that's not been trained enough to join an existing team." Jack nodded as he thought about the thousands of hours of training that would need to take place during the process.

"Ok then team," said Charlie, "why don't we wrap this meeting and get back to our areas and keep up the good work? Mina and Susan, you'll be heading back to Shiloh next week, so we'll need to arrange for a proper send-off."

Kelli's hand shot up as she said 'ooh ooh me me!' Charlie shook his head and smiled. "Ok short round, you're elected send-off chairperson. Just promise me you won't keep demanding to drive the bus, ok?" Kelli feigned a pout and gave Charlie a wink. "No promises your highness." This got Kelli a stare over Charlie's reading glasses.

"Tony, you and I need to head to Carrie's office to review the training plans for the new hires as well as the existing employees when it comes to the kata."

"Sure thing Charlie," said Tony as he got up from the conference room table.

"Hey Thanh, Dean," said Jack, "I want to talk to you guys a bit about your deployment plans over at Shiloh when you have time. Are you both around this afternoon?"

Thanh and Dean looked at each other and nodded with Dean answering "sure thing Jack. We'll swing by after lunch."

"Great, thanks," said Jack.

With that, the group started filing out of the conference room, grabbing their coffee mugs, paper cups, assorted papers, and everything they brought with them. The door closed behind them and the conference room fell silent. A minute later the motion sensor dutifully clicked off the lights.

To be continued....

References and Resources for Improvement Kata and Coaching Kata

Mike Rother's web page shares, for free, all of the resources needed to get started with the kata. There are tools, videos, slideshares... all for free. Just go to this website:

http://www-personal.umich.edu/~mrother/Materials_to_Download.html

You might first want a quick overview of all the concepts and tools by downloading the Kata Practice Kit:

http://www-personal.umich.edu/~mrother/KATA_Files/Kata_Practice_Kit.pdf

Also, Mike's book, Toyota Kata, is a great read and is available through any major outlet.

The Five Question Kata Card

COACHING KATA

The Five Questions

1) What is the **Target Condition**?
2) What is the **Actual Condition** now?

    --------(*Turn Card Over*)----------------->

3) What **Obstacles** do you think are preventing you from reaching the target condition?

    Which *one* are you addressing now?
4) What is your **Next Step**?
   (Next experiment) What do you expect?
5) How quickly can we go and see what we **Have Learned** from taking that step?

*You'll often work on the same obstacle with several experiments

Reflect on the Last Step Taken

Because you don't actually know what the result of a step will be!

1) What did you plan as your **Last Step?**

2) What did you **Expect?**

3) What **Actually Happened?**

4) What did you **Learn?**

-------------------------------->
Return to question 3

The Learner's Storyboard

Focus Process:		Challenge:
Target Condition Achieve by:	Actual Condition Now	PDCA Cycles Record
		Obstacles Parking Lot

Four Steps of the Improvement Kata

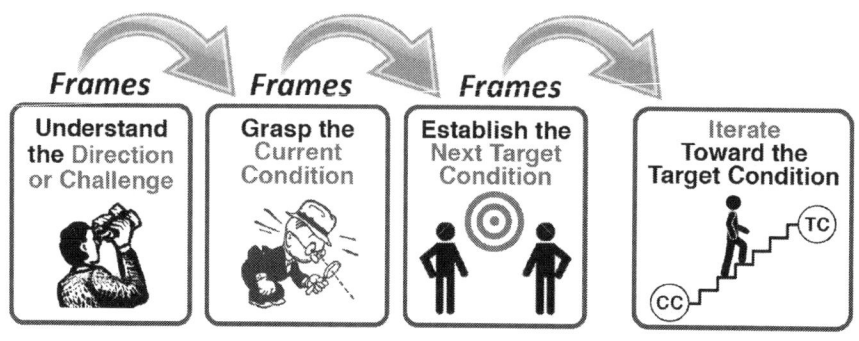

Process Analysis Steps

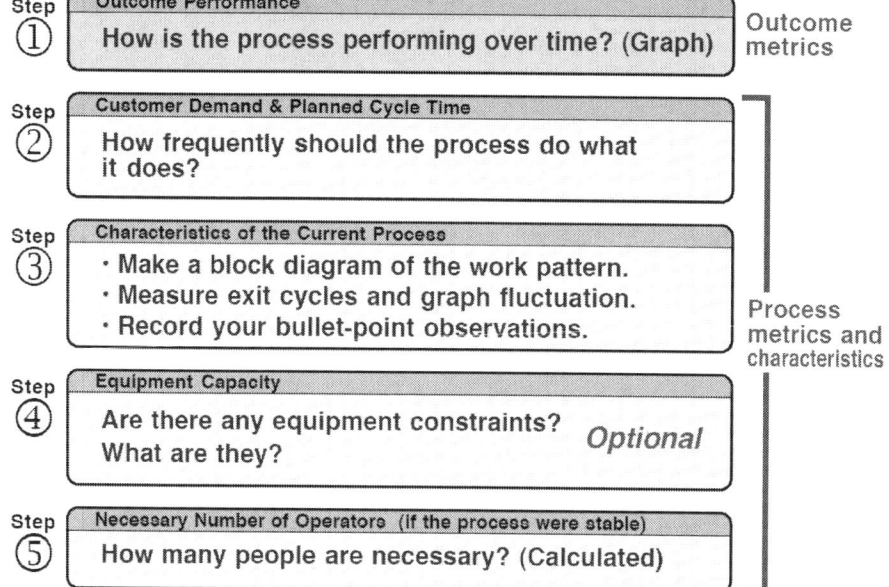

PDCA Cycles Record

Obstacle:	Process:		
	Learner:	Coach:	
Date, step & metric	What do you expect?	What happened	What we learned
		Do a Coaching Cycle / Conduct the Experiment	

(Each row = one experiment)

Online Learning

To take an online, interactive introduction to the Improvement Kata and Coaching Kata you might want to check out the course we created with Mike Rother.

http://www.toyota-way-academy.teachable.com/courses/improvement-kata

ABOUT YOUR AUTHORS

 Shingo Prize-winning author, researcher, and globally recognized lean expert, **James K. Franz** has over 30 years of manufacturing, engineering, and service experience and learned Lean as a Toyota Production Engineer in Japan. He started at the NUMMI plant in California, moved to Motomachi in Japan, repatriating to support Toyota's launch of their second factory in Kentucky.

In 1993, Jim left Toyota to apply his Lean knowledge at Ford Motor Company, beginning in production engineering. In 2000, he accepted a 3-year assignment at Ford of Australia and led their Stamping, Assembly, Casting, and Powertrain facilities to global leadership in Lean. During this time he also worked with Tier 1 and Tier 2 supplier plants in their transformation efforts. Upon his repatriation he became a Lean advisor in Powertrain for global alignment of Lean practices.

Jim left Ford in 2004 to work with twelve-time Shingo Prize-winning author Dr. Jeffrey Liker as a Senior Lean Consultant. In 2008 he partnered with Dr. Liker to co-found the Toyota Way Academy. His work has taken him to over 50 countries and innumerable companies around the globe including Bosch, the U.S. Air Force, Exxon Mobil, AMCOR, Android Industries, Applied Materials, Benteler Automotive, Case New Holland, Caterpillar, Chicago Metallic, Dakkota, Fisher Coachworks, Grand Rapids Chair, Henry Ford Health System, Hertz, JLG, MENLO Logistics, Rio Tinto, SAF Holland, Continental VDO, Visteon, WABCO, and others. He also taught for the University of Michigan's Center for Professional Development's Lean Certification course and has guest lectured around the world as a recognized expert on Lean and Continuous Improvement Cultures and transformation.

Dr. Jeffrey K. Liker is Professor of Industrial and Operations Engineering at the University of Michigan and president of the Toyota Way Academy, a network of top-notch practitioners who consult, coach and teach in the Toyota Way. He is also the president of Liker Lean Advisors.
He is author of the international best-seller, *The Toyota Way: 14 Management Principles from the World's Greatest Manufacturer*, McGraw Hill, 2004 (26 languages, over 850,000 copies sold), and has coauthored six other books about Toyota: *The Toyota Way Fieldbook*, 2005, *The Toyota Product Development System*, *Toyota Talent: Developing exceptional people the Toyota Way*, 2007, and *Toyota Culture: The Heart and Soul of the Toyota Way*, 2008. His three newest books published in 2011 are: *The Toyota Way to Continuous Improvement, Toyota Under Fire: Lessons for Turning Crisis into Opportunity*, and *The Toyota Way to Lean Leadership: Achieving and Sustaining Excellence through Leadership Development*. His newest book is *Developing Lean Leaders at all Levels: A Practical Guide*. His articles and books have won twelve Shingo Prizes for Research Excellence and The Toyota Way also won the 2005 Institute of Industrial Engineers Book of the Year Award and 2007 Sloan Industry Studies Book of the Year. In 2012 he was inducted into the Association of Manufacturing Excellence Hall of Fame and in 2016 inducted into the Shingo Academy.